This book will give you a firm  further into God's promises. *Destiny* website, produces a very comprehensive guide to the developmental process of finding your destiny. We are excited to release this, and I encourage you to dive in and pursue what the Lord has laid out for you.

Banning Liebscher
Director, Jesus Culture, Redding, CA

With the signs of the time upon us – global economic crisis, natural disasters, political upheaval, and hopelessness in the air, *Destiny Finder,* couldn't have come at a better time. There is a generation looking for their reason for existence and Michael Brodeur provides pivotal tools and resources to equip this generation with purpose, direction, and confidence to reach their full God-designed potential and destiny.

Dr. Ché Ahn
Senior Pastor, HROCK Church, Pasadena, CA
President, Harvest International Ministry
International Chancellor, Wagner Leadership Institute

As a songwriter, musician, and worship leader, I find that people have a tendency to try and pigeonhole others to just one thing. The amazing thing about *Destiny Finder* is that it helps you determine and discover who God has called you to be and provides tools to begin and walk out that process. The *Destiny Finder* approach identifies your strengths and giftings and helps to set you on a path to greatness.

William Matthews
Bethel Music recording artist and worship leader

"Who am I?" is a question plaguing a fatherless generation scattered and searching for identity, for destiny, and ultimately for God Himself. Like orphans searching for a father, many desperately desire to discover who they are and what they are called to be. Michael Brodeur has answered the cry of a generation through *Destiny Finder*. This tool prophesies and calls for the gold, the gifts, and the greatness in each and every person who engages in the *Destiny Finder* approach. Users will find that they are able to discover and be the best possible version of themselves.

Shara Pradhan
Co-author, speaker and former assistant to Heidi Baker

I know Michael Brodeur as a faithful pastor through some of the worst warfare a pastor and his family could face, as an astute student of cultural and ethnic networks and how revival can flow through them, and as a Spirit-empowered networker and bridge builder in the Body of Christ. Michael's book *Destiny Finder*, and his website by the same name, will give you a Holy Spirit-inspired, biblical path and bridge to discovering the passionate heart of God and His destiny for you.

This book will show you how God not only intensely loves you and went to the Cross for you, but also how He has a unique destiny — a specific path in life for you — that only you can fulfill with the help and power of His Spirit. In this book, Michael helps you to build a bridge to that Holy Spirit-inspired destiny that God has waiting for you, so that God can bless you to be a blessing (Gen. 12:2) and use you to bring heaven down to earth and to spread His glory and kingdom to every corner of your neighborhood, your city, your state, your country, to the farthest reaches of the planet (Acts 1:8).

Dr. Gary S. Greig
Adjunct Professor of Old Testament, Hebrew, and Prayer and Spiritual Warfare, United Theological Seminary, Dayton, OH

DESTINY FINDER

DESTINY FINDER

Michael Brodeur

Foreword by Banning Liebscher
Director of Jesus Culture

A practical approach to unlocking your destiny

Quintessant Media

Redding, California

Destiny Finder

Copyright © 2012 by Michael Brodeur
Published by Quintessant Media
Redding, CA 96003
www.DestinyFinder.com

First Printing, June 2012
ISBN 978 – 0 – 9856848 – 0 – 8
Cover by Aaron Brodeur, Thought Pool, San Francisco, CA

Printed in the United States of America

My heart is dedicated to you Diane,
my wife of over thirty years and the mother of our seven children. My partner in love, life, and ministry throughout the years, you have shaped me more than any other person on earth. There is nothing that I can do, say, or write that hasn't been flavored by your passionate perspective, your prophetic wisdom and your discerning heart.

To you, Diane, I also dedicate this book.

Contents

ACKNOWLEDGEMENTS

First, I would like to thank my wonderful wife, Diane, and our seven amazing children (and their spouses): Heather (and Chris Strawser), Aaron, Melissa (and Stephen Casey), Christopher (and Claudia Brodeur), Gabriel, Jacob and Michaela. I love each of you and our two beautiful grandchildren, Madeline and Josiah. Our life together has been a great adventure, filled with many challenges and blessings. Through the years, my love and admiration for each one of you has continued to grow and I have no destiny apart from you.

I would also like to thank my ministry partners and friends, Glen Reed and Brian Heltsley, for believing in this project and partnering with me in this vision to help people unlock their destinies.

Thank you to my editorial team, Vicki Wieland, Anna Elkins, Julie Mustard, and especially Lauren Stinton, for your tireless efforts and patience in getting this book from vision to reality. You are each amazing women of God!

My special thanks to Paul Manwaring and Banning Liebscher, two of the many amazing leaders at Bethel

Church in Redding CA. Thanks for believing in me and including me in your worlds. It has been a joy to work with you both to bring the Kingdom of heaven to earth.

Finally, I would like to thank Jesus, the source and the goal of all true destiny.

FOREWORD

Do you know what God's purpose is for your life?

Over the years, I have spoken with hundreds of people who are in the process of discovering who they are and how they fit into God's purpose and plan. Every individual is so unique in personality, gifting, and interest, that I have often thought, there needs to be a more effective way to help people answer some of life's biggest questions. Who am I? What are my spiritual gifts? What are my true passions? What is my destiny? When people know the answers to these questions, they can take deliberate, solid steps toward becoming who the Lord has called them to be.

We live in a culture where most people are raised without a clear sense of identity. They don't know who they inherently are, and as a result, they have a hard time determining where they are going in life. Consequently, many people change their college majors three or four times before graduation, and switch jobs and careers a half dozen times before retirement. Sadly, many end up feeling unfruitful and unfulfilled, but it doesn't have to be this way.

In *Destiny Finder*, Michael Brodeur clearly outlines

how to define your life in a brand new way, how to determine your true identity, and how to see your future with more hope and detail than ever before.

The first step in this exploration process is to understand God has designed you to be entirely unique. He has fashioned every aspect of who you are, with devoted love and intent. He has significant plans for you, and has given you a variety of spiritual gifts to empower you to fulfill His design in and through your life. Michael presents this information in a fresh way you may have not considered before.

Secondly, Michael walks you through discovering the passions the Lord has placed in your heart: the things that drive you, the things that make you excited about living and moving forward—the things that give you life. Once you are able to identify and understand your God-given passions and embrace them, you will find the motivation to keep pursuing His purposes.

The third thing this book does is help you begin to answer the miracle question: If you had no limitations with time, energy, money, or talent, and knew you couldn't fail, what would you do for God? Chances are, your true destiny will be fairly close to your dream.

Finally, Michael offers some practical steps to fulfilling your destiny, including how to access the kind of mentoring and spiritual leadership that will help you grow and become who the Lord has called you to be.

Michael is a relatively new and highly valued member of the Jesus Culture team. He recently joined us to lead our resourcing department in establishing youth and young adults and their leaders to better equip them for revival. Previous to that, he ministered for over thirty years in the city of San Francisco. It was during this time that he began to write the *Destiny Finder* material, testing it over and again with hundreds of people in his Church. To this day, Michael has spiritual sons and daughters all over the world impacting God's Kingdom because of the input they received from he and his team.

If you desire to discover and fulfill what God has called you to do, and are ready to journey toward becoming this person, then I absolutely recommend *Destiny Finder*. This book will give you a firm foundation and propel you further into God's promises.

This book, in tandem with the DestinyFinder.com website, produces a very comprehensive guide to the developmental process of finding your destiny. We are excited to release this, and I encourage you to dive in and pursue the purposes the Lord has laid out for you.

— **Banning Liebscher**
Director, Jesus Culture
Redding, California
May 2012

PREFACE

When I first gave my life to the Lord, it was as if I was being shot out of a cannon. I found Jesus to be so lovely, so worthy and so awesome that the only reasonable response to knowing Him is to give him everything and hold nothing back. As Isaac Watts wrote in his famous hymn, "Were the whole realm of nature mine, that were an offering far too small. Love so amazing, so divine, demands my soul, my life, my all." When I finally "surveyed the wondrous Cross," I offered myself to Jesus as a whole-hearted disciple and did my best to help others to become disciples as well.

However, over the next few years, I realized that that discipleship wasn't as easy as it sounded. Although there were many good discipleship programs out there, they all tended to be either introspective, too controlling or too "cookie-cutter" in their approach. I also soon discovered that many of those who expressed a desire to become disciples, lacked the motivation, the means and the maturity to follow Jesus fully. This realization set me on a journey of prayer and study that eventually led to an understanding of the importance of God's destiny in a person's life.

As I looked at the limitations of different discipleship

programs, I realized that what was needed was a way of helping people grow that was inspiring, personalized and "delight-directed." The Scripture informs us that Jesus was motivated by delight: "... who for the joy that was set before Him endured the cross..." (Heb.12:2b). In the same way, I believe the key to whole-hearted discipleship is to help believers identify the joy set before them, so they can sustain the motivation and means to "take up their crosses and follow" Jesus. This understanding is what eventually gave birth to the "*Destiny Finder*" approach.

Soon after my wife and I started the Vineyard Christian Fellowship church in San Francisco in 1984, I began to develop this tool in the form of a written survey that eventually grew to thirty pages. In the following years, *Destiny Finder* has been used to help hundreds of aspiring believers identify their spiritual gifts and passions, and pursue their God-given dreams. Now, through the power of the Internet, we are able to bring this practical approach to spiritual growth to thousands of people around the world.

This book provides the theological foundations and the personal backstory to help our users get the most out of our online services and resources. My prayer is that you would discover who you are in Christ, where you are going in life and how you can become the person that God has created you to be.

INTRODUCTION

In the 1977 sci-fi film *Close Encounters of the Third Kind*, Richard Dreyfuss plays a character that has an encounter with a UFO and is imprinted with an unshakable vision of an unusual mountain that soon consumes his every thought.

He becomes increasingly preoccupied with the image in his head, and the next morning, we find him shaping this mountain with his shaving cream. At dinner that night, he heaps the mashed potatoes on his plate to attempt to form this mountain. The next day, we see him obsessively molding fifty pounds of modeling clay on the coffee table, and finally, he's digging up his front yard to create a six-foot mountain of garden soil right in the middle of his living room floor, spurring his wife to anxiously gather the children and flee to Grandma's house.

In the midst of all this chaos, he turns his attention to the TV set droning in the background and suddenly sees it on the news broadcast—the mountain he can't get out of his head. In a moment of intense recognition, he sees the real-life expression of the vision that has been placed inside of him, and he drops everything to begin a journey to find this mountain.

Much like this movie character, we are a people who

have experienced a close encounter with the living God. We too have been imprinted with a clear vision, not of an earthly dwelling, but of God's Kingdom. This Kingdom vision has been placed inside every believer, causing us to be consumed with the fulfillment of Jesus' prayer: "Let Your Kingdom come, Your will be done on earth as it is in heaven." Like Abraham, we are "looking for a city that has foundations, whose builder and maker is God." It is our destiny calling to discover our unique role in the fulfillment of this heavenly vision and do what we can in order to bring it to pass on the earth.

God, in His sovereignty, has created each one of us with our ultimate destiny in mind. Every part of who we are — our DNA, our history, our talents, and our truest desires — are all synched up with what God has created us to be and to do. Everything that makes us who we are has been imprinted with God's vision for our future. Yet, just like the character in the movie, until we discover our true destiny orientation, we tend to make messes wherever we go, seeking to fulfill a passion we cannot fully explain.

Why are you on this earth? Why has God created you? Who are you called to be and become? These questions are at the heart of all human longing and aspiration, and when we discover the answers to these questions, we will finally find a life of faithfulness, fruitfulness and fulfillment.

In Ephesians 2:10, the apostle Paul wrote, "We are His workmanship, created in Christ Jesus for good works, which God prepared beforehand that we should walk in them." These "good works" that God has prepared for us are not merely the generic good works that every follower of Jesus is expected to fulfill. They are also the specific works that God has prepared for each individual to accomplish in this life. These good works lie in wait for us — not as some mystical achievement that only a few can obtain, but they are available to us here and now, in the open, if we know how to look for them.

The purpose of this book is to help you discover your personal destiny and fulfill the "good works" which God has created for you. This book will help you identify your gifts and your calling, understand your Kingdom dreams and desires, and figure out how God wants to use you to transform the world.

This book will lead you on a journey to understand who you are in Christ and who Christ is in you. You will discover your new identity, the power of community, your scope of responsibility and your God-given authority in the Lord. You will discover the precious treasure that lives inside of you and in the hearts of those around you.

May this book be a stepping-stone on your incredible journey to freedom, wholeness, passion and purpose.

The destination is worth the pilgrimage.

DestinyFinder.com

The *Destiny Finder* book is a companion to the DestinyFinder.com website. The site contains the Destiny Guide system with online surveys, templates, access to personal coaching, and much more to help you discover and begin to fulfill your destiny. Take the free Destiny Survey to find out your destiny orientation. It reveals your primary core trait that shapes your destiny.

DestinyFinder.com... Unlocking your destiny.

ONE
My Journey / Your Journey

What did you want to be when you were growing up? What were your childhood aspirations? What did you dream about? What stirred you to passion? Every destiny journey begins with the answers to those questions.

As I look back over my life, so many of the things that I dreamed about and did in my early years foreshadowed God's eventual call on me. From an early age, I sensed I had a purpose, and that sense of purpose was visible in my everyday choices and even in the little games I played with my friends. For example, when I was seven years old, I attended a day-care center in the Hunters Point neighborhood of San Francisco. The caretakers would walk us to school in the morning, and my friends and I would break out of the pack and take off running, pretending to be the Beatles running from their fans in *A Hard Day's Night*.

It was just a simple childhood daydream, but in a small way it reflected the destiny God put within me. Even at that young age, I knew that I was meant to influence groups of people, and that sense immaturely manifested in a desire to be one of the Beatles, who were key influencers of the time.

How about you? Maybe you were a child who dreamed about designing clothes or building skyscrapers or being the president of the United States. What did you daydream about when you were young? What did you pretend and act out? How did you spend your playtime?

Though these may seem like childish questions, we should never discount these simple dreams and delights because more often than not, they can be the divine building blocks of our future fruitfulness.

This book is written to help you identify your God-given gifts and calling and combine them with the deep dreams of your heart so that you can discover and fulfill *your personal destiny*. As we begin this journey together, I want to share with you some of my history so that you can begin to understand the dynamics of destiny and apply them to your own life.

Destiny: In the Beginning

I grew up in San Francisco during the 1960's and was an eyewitness to the cultural upheaval of the early hippie scene. In 1967, during the infamous Summer of Love, my best friends lived on Haight and Ashbury, and I spent a lot of time observing the longhaired, strung-out hippie families who made the area their home. From an early age, I was attracted to people who were willing to endure the misunderstanding of others to pursue a counter-culture lifestyle.

My parents divorced when I was still very young, and I lived back and forth between them for most of my unstable childhood. My mom later moved in with a man who was driven by anger and violence and treated us mercilessly. I saw what his abuse did to my sister and brothers, and it birthed within me a desire to change the world by fighting against injustice and abuse. I knew I had to be part of the solution and not a continuation of the problem.

Deeply entrenched in the hippie movement, several years of my childhood were spent living in a communal house, where we smoked pot together every night and took LSD every weekend. Between the ages of thirteen and seventeen, I probably took LSD about three hundred times, and easily, about fifty of those times were with my parents. I established myself as a counter-culture individual, grew my hair out, studied spirituality, and began looking for answers to my own problems and the problems in the world around me.

At first, I thought the answer was political activism. I believed that if I could speak out about racism, war, poverty, and oppression, I could make a difference. My dream for change led to my involvement in almost every anti-war march and political demonstration in San Francisco between 1970 and 1976. Some of these protests turned into riots, and more than once, I had to run and hide and as a line of police dressed in full riot gear marched down the street to quell the demonstrations.

Are you beginning to see a pattern in these stories? Although I was still ignorant and misguided, many of my choices were motivated by a growing sense of calling on my life, a sense of significance: I began to realize that I could make a difference in the world.

This is often how destiny begins to reveal itself in our lives. God, in His sovereignty, has known each of us from the moment of conception and has "wired" each of us in very different ways. Before we knew Him, He knew us and was at work in our lives, putting dreams and desires in our hearts, revealing talents and abilities that would eventually lead us into our individual life callings. Even in the times when we could not fully understand the strong desires that were driving us, God was at work in many of the decisions we made. After all, many of those decisions were in response to the "imprint of the mountain"—a foreshadowing glimpse of the destiny God has given us.

However, while it is true that the seeds of our callings and destinies are sometimes evident in our developmental years, this doesn't mean that there aren't major problems and impurities in our early ideas and actions. In my case, my sense of destiny was certainly mixed with various fears, insecurity, pride, human ambition, and teenage fantasy. I was also subject to the normal patterns of self-centeredness, lust, greed, and a thousand other sinful impulses. Yet in spite of all of these things, I can look back now and see how God was leading me toward Himself and toward the purpose to which He had called me.

From Activist to Seeker

As I progressed through my teens, I began to shift my emphasis from activism to spirituality. I was troubled by the hypocrisy of the activists and protesters I knew, and I was growing increasingly convinced that true global change would never come through demonstrations, elections, and legislation but could come only through the change of the human heart. Although I had already been a student of spiritual things, my exploration began to intensify. I began studying yoga and Tai Chi. I began to meditate on a daily basis and read the writings of a wide array of Hindu, Sufi, Buddhist, and New Age writers. I began a raw foods diet and started fasting up to ten days per month. I was hungry for God.

As I searched for God and learned more about yoga, meditation, and other forms of spirituality, I began to teach what I knew to others. It was a natural step for me because leading and influencing others is part of what God has designed me to do. In my teenage years, I realized I was good at helping people, and I soon became somewhat known as an emerging spiritual leader.

At one point, I joined a group of friends who traveled around the country teaching on spirituality, meditation, and various aspects of eastern philosophy. We led events at the Humanistic Psychology Convention in New Orleans, and we spent a week with the international directors of the YMCA in Boston, teaching them how to integrate eastern philosophy into the YMCA program. Although I was still young on many levels, I was doing what I knew I was meant to do: influencing others and trying to change the world.

I also began regularly hitchhiking across the country, seeking an answer to the questions that were raging within me. These journeys brought me to spiritual gatherings, communes, and communities where other spiritual seekers were pursuing the same answers. Yet with all my searching, I found very few real solutions, and the hunger within me continued only to grow... *There had to be something more.*

A Spiritual Crossroads

At sixteen years old, I reached a significant turning point when I became seriously ill. I originally thought it was the flu so I wasn't too concerned. I didn't go to the doctor right away because, by that time, my family lived about twenty-five miles from the nearest hospital and I was convinced that the symptoms would pass in a day or two. But after ten days, I finally went to the emergency room and found that my appendix had ruptured a week before. I had lost fifty pounds during those ten days and was almost dead.

I ended up staying in the hospital for over a month. The muscles in my arms and legs turned to putty. It was months before I could walk or run again. This experience not only shocked my body but my soul as well. In the midst of this crisis, I began to think about life and death in a new way, and I began to realize how shallow my New Age convictions were and how insufficient they were to answer the true eternal questions of life.

This experience turned out to be a significant turning point in my spiritual journey. It was at this crossroads that I began to lose confidence in the man-made beliefs that I had been pursuing and began to look for something that was deeper, purer, and truer.

God used this near-death experience to help me understand the futility of a purposeless life. A few months after my recovery, I took another important step in my search for significance. I began an internship with a landscape gardener and eventually started my own business. One day, as I was digging a forty-foot irrigation ditch for one of my customers, I had a revelation of the meaninglessness of life. I saw myself forty years in the future still digging ditches, and at that moment I realized there are millions of people who live meaningless lives, digging meaningless ditches to make meaningless money, so they can continue to live meaningless lives. I determined at that moment that I was not going to be one of them. I promised myself that I would discover a purpose worth living for and worth dying for. I ultimately discovered that purpose in Christ.

Driven by the pursuit of purpose, I intensified my search for God inwardly and outwardly, and by the time I was almost eighteen, I had hitchhiked twenty thousand miles all over the United States, Canada, and Mexico. Many of those who picked me up were committed believers and would often take the time to share about their love for Jesus. On one particular day when I was hitching from San Francisco to Mendocino, a woman named Sabine Ball picked me up in a little town called Boonville. Sabine was the leader of a Christian commune called the Lord's Land and was the most infamous "Jesus Freak" in the Mendocino region. She witnessed to me all the way to the coast, telling me about the love of Jesus and the purpose of God for my life. Although I presented my best anti-Christian arguments, I eventually found myself yielding to her words. A few minutes later, as we pulled off the road overlooking the Navarro River, Sabine led me in prayer to receive the Lord Jesus into my heart. It was December 1974.

Do you see the symmetry of my story? Can you see that even in my sin and brokenness, my truest desires and dreams foreshadowed God's ultimate purpose for my life? Even though at the time, I didn't know God, slowly but surely, my aspirations began to match His guidance. He kept leading me in the right direction until I finally gave Him my life, and my destiny became better than anything I could have imagined.

Although I can clearly see the fingerprints of God in my life up to this point, this particular moment changed everything. I was born again, and Jesus began to lead me in ways I had never dreamed about. This is not to say that the next few years were easy. On the contrary, I had no foundation for following Jesus. I had never attended church. I had never read the Bible, and I still believed that Christianity was the lowest form of religious belief on the planet. Still, something had shifted, and God had taken control of my life. In the following chapters, I will share with you some highlights of my life, and hopefully, they will serve as guideposts for your journey to destiny.

Beginning Your Journey to Destiny

As we wrap up this chapter, I encourage you to take a moment and consider your own life. Revisit the questions listed at the beginning of this chapter. What did you want to be as a child? What were your dreams? What were you willing to live for, to fight for, to die for? How have these dreams and desires shaped your journey so far?

This book is designed to be a travel guide and a road map to help you on your journey to the fulfillment of your destiny. Although your personal journey will be different from anyone else's and will be entirely unique to you, I would like to share with you five universal principles that apply to everyone.

Incarnation: You Must Be Born Again

They say that the "journey of a thousand miles begins with a single step." By far, the most important single step in discovering your personal destiny is to receive Jesus as your Savior and Lord. Everything prior to this step is designed by God to bring you to this moment by revealing your deep need and by giving you glimpses of the blessings of new life in Christ.

In the third chapter of John, Jesus makes a profound statement: "Except a man be born again, he cannot see the Kingdom of God." In other words, our personal commitment to Jesus is preliminary to everything else that God has to give us. So, before we journey any further on the road to fulfilling your destiny, why don't you take a moment to confirm your relationship with Jesus.

This message of salvation is simple: God loves you and created you for His glorious purposes. Because of sin and self-centeredness, we have all turned away from God to pursue our own broken purposes. God became flesh and sacrificed Himself to remove the penalty and the power of sin. Through faith in Him, we can be cleansed, forgiven, and receive eternal life. By His grace, we can be transformed by His Spirit to desire what He desires and empowered to fulfill His purposes on the earth. Receiving Him is a simple act of admitting your need, believing that He died for you, turning from your own ways, and embracing His Ways. "But as many as received Him, to them He gave the right to become children of God, to those who believe in His name" (John 1:12).

Once you have received Him as your Savior and Lord, you can begin to see how God was at work in every part of your previous life to bring you to this moment. Once you are born again, His Spirit comes to live inside of you and God once again becomes flesh: incarnation.

Intimacy: Abide in Me and I in You

The second step in the journey to destiny is to begin to build a personal relationship with Jesus through the power of the Holy Spirit. In this process, there are no shortcuts or substitutes. Relationships take time and intention, and relationship with God is no exception. We need to seek His face, hear His voice, study His word, and grow in His grace. Only then will we begin to fully discover who we are in Christ and who He is in us.

Jesus describes the purpose and power of this relationship in John 15:

> "I am the vine and you are the branches...Abide in Me, and I in you. As the branch cannot bear fruit of itself, unless it abides in the vine, neither can you, unless you abide in Me...If you abide in Me, and My words abide in you, you will ask what you desire, and it shall be done for you...By this My Father is glorified, that you bear much fruit; so you will be My disciples."

We are invited to connect with God in such a depth of intimacy and intensity that we become carriers of His presence and conveyors of His power. In the same way as a woman was healed by touching the hem of Jesus' garment, or a handkerchief from Paul was able to expel a demon, God's presence can rest on us and affect reality around us. Just as Peter's shadow healed people on the streets, we are called to carry God's power in a way that changes atmospheres and environments and releases the

Kingdom of God.

God loves you and wants to partner with you in every area of life. God wants to train you to discern His will, to express the gifts of the Holy Spirit, and to "do greater things" than Jesus did because He has gone to be with the Father. God wants to use you to bring blessing and transformation to the world around you, and all this flows out of relationship.

Interdependency: We Are Members of One Another

The next step in the journey to destiny is found in community. We live in a very individualistic culture, and unfortunately some of these attitudes have made their way into the Church. We celebrate the lone ranger and the "self-made man," but ultimately we can never truly know ourselves apart from community, and we can never fully discover and fulfill our destinies apart from community. We need one another. We need to build relationships with fellow believers with whom we can connect, serve, and provide feedback for one another. We best understand who we are in the context of family: the Body of Christ.

In 1 Corinthians 12, the apostle Paul describes our need for one another by using the example of the human body:

> For as the body is one and has many members, but all the members of that one body, being many, are one body, so also is Christ…But now indeed [there are] many members, yet one body…And the eye cannot say to the hand, "I have no need of you"; nor again the head to the feet, "I have no need of you."

Our interdependency is not optional; it is a part of the

very fabric of our relationship with Jesus. We come to Christ as individuals, but our life in Christ is in community. Just as each of us has an individual destiny, we also have a united destiny. And in order for us to walk in our personal mission, we need to remember that we are part of a much bigger mission, which we have come to call the Great Commission.

You are a part of the body, and you need to be activated in the discovery and development of who you are uniquely in Christ so that you are able to bring your necessary gifts to the body. As each part does its share, the body grows. As the body grows, it doesn't just grow in *quantity* but also in *quality*; it edifies itself in love.

Intergenerational: We Need Mentors and Coaches

Another key to the journey of destiny is intergenerational partnership. Just as we need natural mothers and fathers in order to mature in life, we need spiritual mothers and fathers in order to mature in destiny. We live in an orphaned world that is driven by an orphaned spirit. Yet God promised that in the "last days He would send the spirit of Elijah and turn the hearts of the fathers to the children and children to the fathers." This work of restoration is revolutionizing our relationship with our heavenly Father and is also uniting us deeply with spiritual fathers and mothers. God is removing the orphaned spirit by blessing us with anointed pastors, teachers, mentors, and coaches to guide us as we fulfill His purpose on the earth.

Jesus commanded us to "go into all the world and make disciples of all nations . . . teaching them to obey everything that I have commanded." Disciplemaking is spiritual parenting. And just as natural parenting is not complete until your child reaches adulthood, spiritual parenting is not complete until your disciple becomes a disciplemaker.

God is all-sufficient and certainly has everything we need to become all that He has called us to be. Yet in His wisdom, He has determined that His various resources and spiritual nutrients would flow through different sources. Certain nutrients come only through personal encounters with God. Some resources come only through His written word. And still some will come only through anointed leaders. To fulfill our callings in the Lord, we need to align ourselves with godly mentors who can guide us on the journey to destiny.

Intentionality: We Need a Clear Destination

Think of your destiny as a destination on a map. Once you have determined your destination, you need to map your journey within the framework of limited resources: time, energy, money, etc. What is the length of your journey? How often will you need to stop? How much gas will you need? What are the various costs? What about meals, lodging, and unexpected detours? These and other factors require us to be intentional and purposeful in our journey.

The apostle Paul says, "Do you not know that those who run in a race all run, but one receives the prize? Run in such a way that you may obtain it (1 Corinthians 9:24). "Not that I have already attained, or am already perfected; but I press on, that I may lay hold of that for which Christ Jesus has also laid hold of me" (Philippians 3:12).

We all need to set godly goals and share them with

our friends and mentors. We need to place our destinies above every other pleasure, pursuit, and purpose. And we need to press on to apprehend that for which Christ apprehended us.

In the next chapter, we will look at how each of us is created for destiny. This amazing journey begins in the book of beginnings: Genesis, when humanity was created in the image of One who dreams and brings those dreams to pass.

TWO
Created for Destiny

A few weeks after first praying with Sabine to receive Jesus, I had an unusual experience. Sitting on my bed, I was about to begin my morning meditations when I had a vision of three individuals standing before me. I didn't know who they were, and all I could see were their silhouettes. "Are you ready yet?" I heard someone ask. I knew immediately what that question meant: Was I ready to give my life fully to God?

At that moment, I took a serious look at my life. At the time, I was involved in two failing relationships. I was in an aspiring rock band. I was still doing drugs. Although I considered myself a spiritual person, I knew I wasn't ready to give all that up. So I said, "No . . . At least, not yet."

The scene changed, and I saw a shocking image — I saw Jesus on the cross. Because I had no religious background, I had no context for what I was seeing. His flesh was torn, His body bruised, and everything was soaked with blood. He looked at me and said, "When you follow me, it will mean your death."

I knew right away what that meant as well: No more playing games with a convenient spirituality. This was the real thing, and I needed to give my whole life to it. I even needed to be prepared to give my life up for it, if necessary.

That was a life-changing experience for me. At that moment, I started to turn away from the New Age beliefs with all their hypocrisy, and I began to embrace the call to significance that God had placed on my life.

The Importance of Discovering Your Destiny

How do you measure your significance? More importantly, how does God measure significance? In order to understand these kinds of questions, we have to go back to the beginning: the Book of Genesis.

In Scripture, we see that the question of destiny and significance is woven into the very fabric of our DNA:

> Then God said, "Let Us make man in Our image, according to Our likeness; let them have dominion over the fish of the sea, over the birds of the air, and over the cattle, over all the earth and over every creeping thing that creeps on the earth." So God created man in His [own] image; in the image of God He created him; male and female He created them. Then God blessed them, and God said to them, "Be fruitful and multiply; fill the earth and subdue it; have dominion over the fish of the sea, over the birds of the air, and over every living thing that moves on the earth" (Genesis 1:26–28).

God gave us dominion, leadership, responsibility, and stewardship over this planet. He told us to be fruitful, to multiply, and to a certain extent that is what we have done. Over the last several thousand years, humanity has multiplied and filled the earth. Each one of us was created with a hunger for significance and still carries the vestiges of God's original "prime directive." Yet most of us feel cut off from God and frustrated in our efforts to steward even the smallest pieces of our lives. Sensing the responsibility God has given us, we try to have dominion over our little lives, our little cars, our little houses, our families, and our workplaces, not realizing that in the big picture, many of our worries are actually rather miniscule. The reason it is so hard for us to carry this God-given responsibility to reign over the earth is that we face a formidable hindrance: sin.

Our Destiny Was Damaged Through Disobedience

It is impossible for us to overstate the terrible consequences that sin unleashed upon the earth. In Genesis 2:15, we see that God placed Adam and Eve in the Garden of Eden to tend it and keep it. They were given permission to eat of every tree except the tree of the knowledge of good and evil. Along came the serpent, questioning Eve's understanding of God's commandment.

"Did God really say that?" he asked.

Eve answered, "We may eat the fruit of the trees of the garden, but God has said that we cannot eat the fruit of the tree in the midst of the garden, or even touch it, or we will die" (paraphrase of Genesis 3:1–3).

It is interesting that Eve added the words "touch it" because they were not in the original command. So once Eve made the decision and just *removed* the fruit from the tree, she was already open to thinking a bit differently about what God had said.

The serpent said to her, "You won't die!" That is one of the enemy's strategies — to get us to question God's word, which is the first step toward failure in our lives. The serpent continued:

> "For God knows that in the day you eat of it your eyes will be opened, and you will be like God, knowing good and evil." So when the woman saw that the tree [was] good for food, that it [was] pleasant to the eyes, and a tree desirable to make [one] wise, she took of its fruit and ate. She also gave to her husband with her, and he ate (Genesis 3:5-6).

Afterward, their eyes were opened; they knew they were naked, and they covered themselves in fig leaves for one purpose- to hide.

By disobeying, they sinned and separated themselves from God. It was not just a separation from His presence, but it was also a separation from His *purposes* for humankind and from the very destiny He created us to fulfill. Sin caused a breach in the very order of creation.

How does this affect our pursuit of destiny? Adam and Eve were created to rule and reign on God's behalf. They were created with a significant purpose. Humanity is not simply a plaything or a novelty for God; we have been created with a divine job description. This is just as true today as it was with Adam and Eve.

Sin Introduced Shame and Guilt

God walked through the garden, and Adam and Eve tried to hide themselves from His presence. Creation tried to hide from the Creator. Why would Adam and Eve do that? Why would *we* do that? What usually holds us back from God? Most likely, it is feelings of guilt and shame, which lead us to feel disconnected from and unaccepted by God. We feel disconnected because of the root sin, and then we feel unaccepted because we know that there are things we have done in our lives that are contrary to His heart. Yet the call to destiny was never revoked.

"Where are you?" God called to Adam (Genesis 3:9–11).

"I heard Your voice," Adam answered, "and I was afraid because I was naked; and I hid myself."

Do you think God really needed to know where Adam was? God's question was not about Adam's location but about the intimate connection that had been severed because of disobedience. God's question was provoking Adam and Eve to think about why they felt it necessary to hide and clothe themselves. Before sinning, Adam and Eve hadn't even noticed they were naked. After the sin, they noticed and were ashamed.

Sin Introduced the Blame Game

Adam answered God by blaming Eve: "The woman whom You gave [to be] with me, she gave me of the tree, and I ate" (Genesis 3:12). And thus began the pattern of blame shifting that has raged for thousands of years and caused strife and additional separation. Instead of taking responsibility for his actions, he said the equivalent of, "Somebody made me do it," just as we often do to this day.

It is important to understand what causes this to happen in our lives today. Later, we will look at family relationships and whether our childhoods empowered or hindered us in the area of blame, but whatever the case, we must avoid blame at all costs. An important step in embracing destiny is taking responsibility for who we are and the choices we make. Even when we make a bad choice, we must realize that taking responsibility for our own actions empowers us to walk in the direction of, and fulfill, our destinies.

Because of Adam and Eve's disobedience, God told Adam:

"And I will put enmity
Between you and the woman,
And between your seed and her Seed;
He shall bruise your head,
And you shall bruise His heel."

To the woman He said:
"I will greatly multiply your sorrow and your
conception;
In pain you shall bring forth children;
Your desire [shall be] for your husband,
And he shall rule over you" (Genesis 3:15-16).

Fruitfulness Would Now Be Difficult

A multitude of profound problems emerged from this original disobedience, but perhaps the saddest consequence of sin was the division of man and woman and the pain that would now accompany childbearing. God had called us to be fruitful and multiply, but now fruitfulness would come at a high cost. One of the key elements of our destiny would now be hindered.

There Would Be Division and Disunity

The next problem stems from the division and disunity caused by sin between Adam and Eve. In God's original command, their relationship was intended for coleadership, but now their equality would experience tension. God told Eve, "Your desire shall be for your husband." That actually means that her desire would be to control him, yet he would rule over her.

Woman was placed in an inferior position with an indwelt unction to usurp that role. Thus, the male-female power struggle began. Another key element of destiny would now be hindered.

Then God told Adam:

> "Because you have heeded the voice of your wife, and
> have eaten from the tree of which I commanded you,
> saying, 'You shall not eat of it':
> "Cursed [is] the ground for your sake;
> In toil you shall eat [of] it a
> All the days of your life.
> Both thorns and thistles it shall bring forth for you,
> And you shall eat the herb of the field.
> In the sweat of your face you shall eat bread
> Till you return to the ground,
> For out of it you were taken;
> For dust you [are],
> And to dust you shall return" (Genesis 3:17–19).

Another terrible consequence of human sin was the frustration of labor. Before the fall, there was abundance in every area of life, but after the fall, our resources would be limited and prosperity would come only through toil. A third key element of our destiny would now be hindered.

What Does This Mean Today?

Here's the challenge: God gave humanity a clear mandate to multiply and fill the earth and have dominion over it, causing it to blossom into His purposes. However, the plan was perverted, and instead we have a world that is ruled by division, strife, war, greed, poverty, and so forth.

As a result of human disobedience, both aspects of God's plan—*blessing* on the earth and *multiplication* on the earth—were hindered. Although the desire for blessing and increase was never taken away, the fulfillment of destiny became a painful process, one that requires more than human effort to fulfill.

It is important to remember that, as a result of the Fall, our destiny plan was not entirely destroyed but merely damaged. The inner, God-given impulse to "multiply, fill the earth and subdue it" was still intact, but this innocent aspiration to rule and reign as God's stewards of this planet became twisted into selfish ambition to possess and control. A call to destiny that is cut off from an abiding relationship with God will inevitably degenerate into competition, conflict, and control.

God Has Restored Our Destinies in Jesus

Thankfully, God didn't leave the story there; He set in motion a restoration plan that began with Abraham and extended through the generations to His Son, Jesus, and now to us. This amazing plan of God not only restores us to *relationship* with Him by removing the barrier of sin, but it also restores us to the *partnership* that God has always intended. This partnership is expressed in seven billion different ways according to the unique design and destiny that God has given each of us.

In Ephesians, Paul details God's awesome plan to redeem us from our depravity and restore us through His love and mercy. His recovery plan for the planet wasn't a one-time overhaul—but an individual restoration process.

He reaches out to each of us and brings us back into relationship with Himself in a way that allows us to rediscover and reclaim our destinies. In so doing, He empowers us to be the change agents to restore our planet.

God specifically emphasizes His restoration plan in Ephesians 2:8, where Paul says, "For by grace you have been saved through faith." His grace is a gift I have to receive *first*—before I walk in the other gifts. It is the prerequisite. And what a wonderful gift it is! We get to accept the mercy and restoration of God and not rely on our imperfect human efforts. This journey toward destiny is not something we could do ourselves. We need Him and His grace, and He is very willing with both.

> "[It is] the gift of God, not of works, lest anyone should boast. For we are His workmanship, created in Christ Jesus for good works, which God prepared beforehand that we should walk in them" (Ephesians 2:8-10).

In other words, *we* are His work; He is working in us and on us. He is working to mobilize and empower His people to go out and be witnesses of who He is. That is our mission.

Beginning the Discovery Process

As we have just begun to see, the Book of Ephesians is about the destiny journey, beginning with a long series of statements about our identity in Christ. *His* identity is the source of *our* destiny. If you don't know who you are, you will not know where you are going, and you will certainly not know how to get there. In any journey, the point of origin is the first thing you have to know. In order to go somewhere, you have to know where you are going to start.

Say someone tells you, "Go three blocks and turn left, then go three blocks and turn right." If you don't know where you are starting from, those specific directions will lead you to a variety of places, with a very small chance that any of them will be the correct destination. However, once you know your starting point, you can chart your course with confidence on any kind of journey.

In the first chapter of Ephesians, Paul provides us with an amazing foundation for who we are in Christ. First, we find that we have been blessed with every spiritual blessing in Jesus (verse 3). Then we discover how He has chosen us in Him before the foundations of the world that we should be holy. We are chosen—picked out on purpose for a purpose (verse 4). Next, the apostle affirms that we are predestined to adoption as sons, who have been fully accepted in the Beloved One (verses 5–6).

These are all preliminary truths leading to the point of reconciliation in the following four verses:

> In Him we have redemption through His blood, the forgiveness of sins, according to the riches of His grace which He made to abound toward us in all wisdom and prudence, having made known to us the mystery of His will, according to His good pleasure which He purposed in Himself, that in the dispensation of the fullness of the times He might gather together in one all things in Christ, both which are in heaven and which are on earth—in Him (Ephesians 1:7-10).

God's eternal purpose is to restore all things to their original intended state by gathering them together and placing them under the loving leadership of Jesus Christ.

Paul goes on to say that we have been granted an awesome inheritance (verse 11) and that we have been sealed with the Holy Spirit of promise (verse 13). As the chapter concludes, Paul begins to pray over the Church that God would give them a spirit of wisdom and revelation and the knowledge of Him (verse 17). Our destinies are directly tied to God—we do not have true destiny apart from Him.

Paul wants to open the eyes of our understanding that we may comprehend certain things. First, he prays that we would receive the *spirit of wisdom*. Wisdom is the ability to take knowledge and apply it in a clear and effective way. Next, he prays that we would receive the *spirit of revelation*. Revelation is the direct download of information and perspective from God through the Holy Spirit. We need both wisdom and revelation if we hope to fulfill God's purposes on the earth. In wisdom and revelation we see the combination of the Word and Spirit working together in our lives and circumstances. Wisdom comes from the Word being applied to our lives, and revelation comes from direct relationship with the Holy Spirit.

Finally, Paul prays that the eyes of our understanding would be enlightened to comprehend three specific things:

- That we would know the hope of His calling,

- That we would know the riches of the glory of His inheritance in the saints, and

- That we would experience the exceeding greatness of His power.

The Hope of His Calling

God's calling is that we would be with Him, completely restored, forever and ever throughout all eternity. We call this Eternal Life, which, contrary to popular belief, does not begin after we die. It begins the moment we accept Jesus. Eternal life is not only about living forever, but it is also a *quality* of life that begins now. This quality of life is intended to increase for the rest of our earthly lives and continue on into the afterlife.

So as Paul is praying that we would know the hope of His calling, he is referring to the eternal call that begins right now and unfolds throughout our lives until we go to be with Him forever. He is actually praying that we would discover our God-given destinies: a revelation of whom we *are* in God (our identity) and who we *are called* to be in Him (our destiny).

God has a unique design for each one of us. Our eternal destiny is ultimately a culmination of our earthly destiny — an expression of the specific design of God in us. Understanding the relationship between our earthly and eternal destiny requires both wisdom and revelation. Paul prays that we will know these things with certainty in our hearts and that we will begin to pursue them right now.

It is essential that we grasp the *hope* of God's calling in our lives before we move ahead. Our calling is like a great treasure chest of gold that God has placed within us to be spent on His purposes. Once we discover it, we must embrace it. In order to discover it, we must organize your life, priorities, and purposes around the fulfillment of the calling that God has given you.

The Glory of His Inheritance in the Saints

Following the prayer for wisdom, revelation, and calling, Paul prays that we may know "the riches of the glory of His inheritance in the saints" (Ephesians 1:18).

Paul is famous for his run-on sentences, and sometimes it can be easy to miss what he is really trying to say. In this case, Paul wants us to know how rich the glory of our inheritance is. Then he informs us *where* our inheritance can be located: It can be found "in the saints." In other words, the inheritance that you and I are receiving from God is embedded in believers all around us and around the world. This means that I will never receive my full inheritance from God until I discover the treasure that God has placed in you and other people.

I want to make this as clear as possible. On a personal level, I must first understand my calling and the treasure God has placed in me. Then I can help those around me understand the hope of *their* callings and the treasure God has placed in them. Once we all discover our callings and the treasure hidden within us, we can begin to draw out the gold in one another and bask in the wealth of the Body of Christ. As we all dig deep into our hearts and discover the hidden gold that lies within, we will have limitless resource to love one another and love the world around us.

As I am assured of my calling in the Lord and start living my life with that sense of identity, I can also be assured that everyone *around* me also has a calling. When I can see that *my* inheritance from God is buried in them, it becomes my life mission to dig out from my brothers and sisters the treasure that God has hidden inside of them.

As the parable says, the man who discovered treasure in a field sold everything he possessed to buy the whole field to dig out the treasure. It is important to remember that people are just people, and when we are dealing with people, there will be times when it will seem like there is a lot more "field" than "treasure." Gold mining is hard work, and sometimes it can seem like a losing proposition. Stories exist of miners who gave up on a particular mine when they were within three feet of the mother load.

We need to remind ourselves that the riches of the glory of God are embedded in each believer. We may have to clear a lot of dirt and blast through a lot of rock to bring that glory to the surface. As we learn how to help others remove the pain and problems that hinder them and get down to the deep gold that is buried within, we will be rich beyond our imagination. Again, we do not uncover the gold in others' lives solely because it is good for them; we also do it because it is good for us—our lives become better as their lives become better. God created us to need one another.

God is at work in all of us to draw out the destiny possibilities in others. The wealth that we possess is linked to the destiny that each of us is discovering and developing in Christ.

The Exceeding Greatness of His Power

Paul concludes by praying that we would know "the exceeding greatness of His power toward us who believe, according to the working of His mighty power" (Ephesians 1:19). Another way of stating this threefold prayer is that God wants you to know the power He has placed in you, the power He has placed in other believers, and the power that He has made available to defeat darkness and release His Kingdom on the earth.

When Paul begins to describe the power that God has made available to us, he says that it is according to the mighty power that God worked in Jesus Christ when He raised Him from the dead and seated Him at His own right hand. The same resurrection power that raised Jesus from the grave and exalted Him to the highest place is dwelling inside of you and me. If we can come into a revelation of that power, things will change.

Think about it: That same power exalted Jesus above all principalities, power, might, dominion, and every name that can be named — not only in this age but also in the age to come. This is the supreme power of God that was unleashed in Jesus Christ when God raised Him from the dead. This is the same power that dwells in each of us! In the same way that God has put all things under Jesus' feet, He has put all things under our feet as well.

Because the Church has not always understood or embraced this power, we have settled for a quality of life that is far below what Jesus has given us, and as a result, we have failed to influence and impact the world as Jesus intended. Instead, we have developed theologies that justify our powerlessness and have even, at times, confused the power of God with the power of the devil. This lack of understanding about the power of God has led many to conclude that we are at best perpetual sinners who, though saved by grace, will never amount to much. But God has called us to be more than conquerors through Him who loves us. We are His champions on the earth. God has ordained us to carry His transforming power throughout the earth, bringing restoration, salvation, healing, and deliverance.

We Have Been Created for Destiny

God created humanity to rule and reign with Him on the earth, but our destiny was damaged through disobedience, and we released the consequences of sin upon the earth. In the death and resurrection of Jesus, a new humanity was born that restored God's rule and reign in the earth and restored us to the original destiny that God gave us.

In addition to being part of a new humanity, you are also personally a new creation (2 Corinthians 5:17), specially destined by God to accomplish certain things that will give Him glory and give you the deepest fulfillment. Depending on this unique design of God in your life, you may walk out your destiny as a mother raising children, as the CEO of a company, as a movie producer, as a carpenter or athlete, as a politician, etc. God desires to manifest Himself in every sphere of society, every daily occupation, and every arena of life.

Many mistakenly believe that unless they are pastoring a church or preaching at conferences, they have no significant role in the eternal purposes of God. But really the contrary is true. Only a small percentage of believers will ever be paid "clergy," but all of us are called to be ministers. Most of the world-changers in Scripture were not professional priests but carpenters, fishermen, tax collectors, and political leaders.

Every true believer in Jesus has been born again and is filled with the resurrection power of Jesus Christ. Every one of us has been given a sphere of influence in which we can bring blessing and transformation. Each of us has been given spiritual gifts, dreams, and desires that match the sphere to which we are called. Each of us will only be fruitful and fulfilled in life to the degree to which we discover our destinies and fulfill our life callings.

As we begin to engage this discovery process, we must realize that it actually is a multi-step process. The first step is that of beginning to understand our identity; this is followed by making our calling and election sure and finally by understanding God's calling and election in the lives of the people around us, which maximizes the fact that God has placed resurrection power inside each one of us.

If we will believe and walk in that resurrection power, we will not fail to bring God's Kingdom to earth.

THREE
Destiny: Redeeming Our History

About six months after my initial salvation experience, I was hitchhiking through the Northwest on my way to the Rainbow Gathering. I had just attended a Hopi Peyote Ceremony for the healing of the earth in Vancouver, B.C., and was looking forward to camping in the wilderness with 25,000 spiritual seekers called the Rainbow People.

Although I had already prayed to receive Jesus and had experienced a taste of His presence, I still had no foundation in God at this point. My approach to God was along these lines: *Okay, Jesus. If You're real, make Yourself real to me.* So one day on the road, while standing on a lonely freeway onramp, I began to pray, "Please lead me to a place where I can find out about You." At this stage of my life, I didn't care what religion it was, just so long as it was real.

After a few days of travel, I ended up on the Blackfeet Indian Reservation in Montana where I crossed paths with a dark-skinned man as he was walking out of the Browning General Store. He had long black braids and was covered with Indian jewelry. I introduced myself, and he told me his name was Tinyman Heavyrunner. He seemed friendly, but when I asked him if he knew where the Rainbow People were gathering, he quickly shushed me and told me to get into his car. "Don't talk about the Rainbow Gathering. The Indians don't like it."

So I did as he said, and as we began to drive, he explained to me that the Indians didn't like the Rainbow People because the attendees were a bunch of upper middleclass white people who were pretending to be Indians. But Tinyman went on to explain that he liked hippies and that he was not your average Indian; he was in touch with the outside world and considered himself a progressive. He lived in a teepee and was a teacher of the Indian way at the local high school.

Tinyman drove me around for over an hour trying to find a friend who knew the location of the Rainbow. But the day was growing dark, and he finally invited me to spend the night at his place. We drove south out of Browning toward Heart Butte and stopped midway, turning right on a little dirt road that led to a homestead nestled up against the rise of the Rocky Mountains. I went to sleep that night in Tinyman's teepee thinking that God had brought me there to learn the Indian Way . . . but actually God had a very different plan.

The next day, I left for the Rainbow Gathering and was gone for about a week. But I soon grew bored of the Rainbow crowd, and decided to go back to Browning and stay a little while longer with my new friend. Tinyman took me to his family camp and that was where I first met the couple who permanently changed my life- Albert and Agnes Wells, Tinyman's grandparents, and radical followers of the Lord Jesus.

Albert was born around the turn of the twentieth century and had grown up on the reservation amidst great poverty and pain. As a child, he attended Catholic mission schools, where he was forced to eat soap if he spoke in his native tongue. When he failed to obey their rules, he was stretched out, tied to a fence, and beaten. This happened on a regular basis because of his inability to comply with the mission's expectations. Obviously, none of this gave him a very good impression of Jesus. He became an alcoholic and began to drink excessively.

As a result of his familiarity with rotgut liquor, he began to pass blood on a continual basis and was told by the doctor that his stomach lining was destroyed; he didn't have long to live. So he went to a bar to drink himself to death.

While he was in the bar with about thirty other people, Jesus appeared, standing on a barroom table! Everybody saw Him. People screamed and yelled, ran out of the bar, and dove under tables.

Jesus stood there and said to him, "Sober up and follow Me." He turned to Agnes, Albert's wife, and said, "Fast for four days, and your husband will be healed. I have called you to an amazing ministry."

Albert's brother, Arthur, who was in the bar that day, confirmed this story. He told me that when Jesus appeared, he screamed, dropped his drink, and ran out of the bar as fast as he could. What is interesting is that Arthur did not come to the Lord for several more years. But when he finally did, he followed in his brother's footsteps by becoming an evangelist to the Native American Peoples throughout North America.

For forty years after this visitation, God used Albert Wells in amazing ways. By the time I met him, he had seen hundreds of people healed and saved. God used him in spiritual warfare among the witch doctors and shamans on the land. It was an amazing privilege for me—this young hippie kid—to be discipled by this man. Everyone referred to Albert as the Old Guy. When I met him, he was in his mid 70's and semi-retired from ministry. Albert took me in and invited me to stay with his family on the land. He later told me that Jesus had spoken to him when I first arrived and said, "This is My son Michael. You're supposed to take him in and care for him, for I have called him to serve Me."

When I accepted the Wells' invitation to live with them, I had no idea what I was getting myself into, but God did. It took me a few days to realize that the Old Guy and his wife were true followers of Jesus. They were different from any other Christians I had ever met, and it ended up being the perfect bridge for me. I began to learn about God in a way that made sense to my open-ended, counter-culture mindset. God had arranged the steps of my destiny so He could build within me the firm foundation I did not yet have.

I began to hear the Old Guy's stories and meet people who had been healed through his ministry. In terms of regular religion, he was clearly out of the box, but he was one of the most spiritual people I had ever met. He was very primitive and almost entirely illiterate. He had learned the Scriptures through seven separate visitations of Jesus. Yet he walked in the presence and power of God in a mighty way.

During my time with the Indians, I decided I would read through the whole Bible. As I read about the great men and women in Scripture, I thought, *Wow. God called all of these different people to serve Him in so many powerful ways.*

What's my calling? Who am I? What have I been gifted to do for God?

Fall changed to winter, and I moved from the teepee to an army tent with a wood stove and an electric blanket. (They had electricity but no running water). The more I read the Bible stories, the more I started to obsess on the topic of destiny. I sought the Lord: "God, I must have a calling. Reveal my destiny to me!"

One night, I attended an awkward little revival meeting in the Wells' house. I must admit I came to the meeting with a bad attitude. I was bothered by everything that night. I was bothered by the fact that everyone around me was singing off key. I was bothered by a certain young religious guy who was showing off his knowledge of Scripture. Most of all, I was bothered by my bad attitude. Fed up with myself, I prayed, *God, please help me!*

Then the Spirit of God began to move in the room. A woman who had been horribly bound began coughing and gagging as she threw up a gelatinous black ball the size of a grapefruit. She was instantly set free from demonic control.

Suddenly, I was overcome by a flow of love like nothing I had ever experienced. I felt like I loved everyone in the room, which was a very different emotion than what I had been feeling for them a few minutes before!

As this amazing meeting drew to a close, I decided it was time for me to hear from God. I went outside, away from the house and into the freezing cold night, and lay face down in the dirt. I determined that I was not going to get up from there until God revealed to me my destiny.

Almost an hour passed. I heard the people leaving the meeting. Then suddenly, after a long silence, I heard a loud voice speaking to me. The only problem was that I couldn't understand the words because they were in the Blackfeet language. Embarrassed, I got up quickly, brushed myself off, and looked around to see who had been speaking. No one was there.

I walked into the house and told the Old Guy what had happened. He said he didn't know what this meant, but he asked Agnes to pray and ask the Lord about it.

Agnes went outside to pray and came back with a word from the Lord for me. "That was the Lord speaking to you, and He wants you to know that He has a great calling and ministry for you, and it will unfold over many years. You will be a leader among His people, and you will do signs and wonders, and you will lead many to faith. For the time being, He wants you to lead praise and worship."

Little did I know that my quest for destiny would lead me from there into a life of commitment and dedication that was almost the opposite of the life I had lived before. As I encountered God in that moment, I felt like I was standing on the rim of the Grand Canyon, about to dive into the Colorado River. God was preparing me for a life of influence and impact that would require everything I was.

God Turns Our Mess into Our Message

Today, I can look back and see that my history was preparation for my destiny. At first glance, it might seem like there is a great contrast between my history and my destiny, and in some ways, that is true. I went from being a counter-culture kid who couldn't stay in one place longer than six months to being a married man ministering in one city for over thirty years. In fact, Diane and I and our seven children ended up living in the same house for over twenty-seven years! If you had told me in my teens that I would end up staying in one place for so long, I would have laughed. By the grace of God, I have been empowered to walk out a living faith, not allowing the hurts and abuses of the past to run my life. By God's grace, I was able to replace areas of pain, hopelessness, disillusionment, and instability with healthy structures for my family. I learned the value of roots and structure to security and health.

Yet in many other ways, my history was a perfect preparation for my destiny. I received a wide exposure to different political and philosophical beliefs that has enabled me to communicate with a wide variety of people. I experienced instability and abuse that prepared me to minister to diverse kinds of people with a wide range of personal issues. I had to adapt to a myriad of new environments and relationships, which has helped me to have a broad ability to multi-task and manage a multitude of variables in life. I was raised in a city on the cutting edge of culture, and I am called to affect emerging culture.

How has your history prepared you for your destiny? How has your family of origin — biological or adopted — played a part? How have you been shaped by the positive and negative experiences of your childhood? As we grow in our pursuit of destiny, we grow in our ability to see how God can redeem every part of our lives for His purposes. You might be thinking, *"My life is so messed up. How could I ever hope to have a destiny in God?"* I thought the same thing about myself for a long time. But thankfully, God is bigger than our messes.

God Works All Things Together for Good

If you have given your life to God, you are His son or daughter. His Spirit has been implanted inside you, and He is transforming you.

We are changed by His majesty and are continually being transformed into His image. We are empowered to become the person He has determined we will become.

Although it may seem like an impossible miracle, God intends to redeem every aspect, even the most painful, for our good and for His glory. He didn't ordain the pain, but He will work all things together for good to those who love Him and who are called to His purpose.

We see a clear example of His intentions and promises in the story of Joseph.

Joseph's History Foretold His Destiny

Jacob loved his son Joseph. He favored this child of his wife Rachel and made him a coat of many colors. I have a feeling that Joseph was probably a little spoiled. Certainly, his ten half-brothers thought he was, and they became extremely jealous of him. The Bible tells us that Joseph's brothers "hated him and could not speak peaceably to him."

In Genesis 37, we read that Joseph had two dreams. In the first, he and his brothers were out in the field, and their sheaves bowed down to his sheaf.

After hearing the dream, his brothers said to him, "Shall you indeed reign over us? Or shall you indeed have dominion over us?" So they hated him even more for his dreams and for his words.

In the second dream, Joseph saw the sun and moon

and eleven stars bowing down to him. This time, even his father rebuked him. "What is this dream that you have dreamed? Shall your mother and I and your brothers indeed come to bow down to the earth before you?"

Clearly, neither dream went over too well with Joseph's older brothers. They resented him for his dreams and began to plot his demise.

One day, Joseph was called to bring food to his brothers out in the field. They saw him coming and hatched a plan. They decided they were going to kill him.

They threw him into a pit, planning to leave him there to die. But then, fortunately for Joseph, they saw a caravan on its way to Egypt and decided to make a profit instead. They sold him into slavery. In an instant, Joseph went from dreaming himself king over his brothers to being someone's property.

Once the transaction was complete, his older brothers took Joseph's coat of many colors, sprinkled it with blood, and returned home with news for their father: "Joseph was killed by an animal! See? Here's the blood on his coat."

Their father wept, utterly heartbroken, and the brothers thought they were finished with Joseph forever.

In Egypt, Joseph was sold to a man named Potiphar. The boy was so faithful and hardworking that Potiphar eventually placed him in charge of his entire house. Everything was going well until Potiphar's wife decided she fancied Joseph. She attempted to seduce him, and when he rejected her, she became angry, accused him of rape, and he was thrown into prison.

Joseph Was Victimized But Never Became a Victim

If the story ended here, it would be a miserable end to

a miserable life, especially since his early dreams were so dramatically opposite of his prison reality. In Joseph's childhood, God had shown him something great—a destiny of leadership over his family. Now, everything in his life had shifted. Instead of becoming the ruler of his family, he lost his position, his father's name, and his freedom. He was assigned to the lowest position in the land.

I think that many of us can relate to Joseph. We have been given dreams and promises from the Lord, but miserable circumstances have come on the heels of those dreams, and we find ourselves gripped by discouragement and doubt. From this vantage point, it is hard to see how our painful circumstances are ever going to morph into the destiny God has shown us. We wonder, *How is God possibly going to do what He has promised? Does He not see what I'm going through here?* Many of us forget that we have a great calling and destiny on our lives because so far, all we have seen is disappointment and discouragement.

Joseph was a man with a dream, but he was also a man who endured great difficulty; he was a victim of his circumstances. Have you ever felt that way? Have you ever sat back, considered your future destiny against your present situation, and concluded that God may care about others but He does not care about you?

I believe that many of us miss the fact that God sees and understands what we are going through. In Luke 4:18, humanity is described as poor, brokenhearted, captive, blind, and oppressed. Matthew 9:35–38 says that Jesus saw the masses as sheep weary and scattered, without a shepherd, and He was moved with compassion for them.

God remembers our frame; He knows that we are dust

(Psalm 103:14). From a natural perspective, Joseph had no hope whatsoever—but in this story, God proves that no one's dream is out of His hands.

God's Restoration

Joseph finally ended up getting his big opportunity, but it came years after his original dream.

While Joseph was in prison, Pharaoh's chief baker and chief cupbearer offended their lord and were imprisoned in the house of the captain of the guard, where Joseph was confined. Each man had a dream that Joseph correctly interpreted: The baker was later executed, and the cupbearer was reinstated to Pharaoh's service.

Joseph asked the cupbearer, "Please remember me to Pharaoh. I am here innocently." For the first time, Joseph had hope. No doubt he thought, *Finally, I am about to be helped!* But the cupbearer forgot about him, and he remained in prison for two more years.

At the end of those two years, Pharaoh had two dreams. He sought counsel from all the priests and magicians, but no one could interpret them. It was then that the cupbearer finally remembered Joseph. I can imagine him slapping his hand to his forehead and saying, "That reminds me! A couple of years ago, I met this guy who could interpret dreams." So Joseph was brought into Pharaoh's presence.

When asked to interpret the dreams, he responded, "It is not in me, but God will give Pharaoh an answer of peace." Joseph correctly interpreted the dreams of the cows and wheat to mean that there would be seven years of plenty in Egypt followed by seven years of famine.

Pharaoh was impressed. He ended up appointing

Joseph as manager over his entire kingdom, and along with his other duties, Joseph found himself overseeing the stocking of grain silos. Sure enough, the seven years of plenty passed and then came the famine. This famine covered the entire region, and Joseph's family began to be in need. You know the rest of the story: His brothers came to buy food, Joseph recognized them, and eventually he revealed himself as their long-lost brother.

Choice in the Challenges

Like Joseph, you might have a painful family history. You might have endured verbal or physical abuse, possibly worse. Even small injuries can impact our souls in ways that cause woundedness, and if we don't deal with that woundedness, it will eventually sabotage our destinies. Victimization and the self-pity that can follow are responsible for derailing many God-given destinies. If Joseph had allowed hurt and woundedness to overcome him, he might never have fulfilled his destiny and reconciled with his family — but he did, and in the process, he discovered that God was at work in the midst of his challenges.

So what happened to Joseph's dreams? They ultimately all came true. His family *did* bow to him. After their father died, the brothers said, "Perhaps Joseph will hate us, and may actually repay us for all the evil which we did to him." So they sent a messenger to him, reminding him of their father's words of restoration and forgiveness. Then they came into his presence and bowed low before him, declaring, "We are your servants."

Joseph's response to his brothers' plea for forgiveness

is beautiful: "You meant evil against me; [but] God meant it for good, in order to bring it about as [it is] this day, to save many people alive" (Genesis 50).

We may suffer pain, disappointment, even terror, but we have the opportunity to choose our response: Will we become victims of this pain, or will we walk through it in a way that brings us healing and allows us to move forward into our dreams and destinies?

I have heard people who were raised in upper middle-class homes complain about how bad their childhoods were. On the other hand, I have also read the stories of survivors of the Nazi concentration camps who are the most thankful people on earth. What is the difference? The difference was in their responses to their circumstances. Ultimately, it is not my circumstance but how I *respond* to my circumstance that defines me. What will define you?

Here, however, we have to be careful. Did God inspire Joseph's brothers to sell him into slavery? Did God inspire Potiphar's wife to accuse him falsely of rape? The answer to both questions is an emphatic "No!" God is good, and He loves us. People do bad things, but God can turn bad into good.

Yes, He can do a great work in us in the midst of hardship and pain, but He does not *choose* to throw bad situations on us to "work on our character" or "teach us a lesson." Joseph came to a place where he saw his pain and challenging circumstances through God's eyes. He saw that in spite of his brothers' sin, in spite of the sin of Potiphar's wife, in spite of the calamities he endured, God used everything to guide him to a place where his dream could be fulfilled.

God Redeems History to Fulfill Destiny

God is intent upon redeeming your history so that you can fulfill your destiny. In fact, the redemption of your history is one of the foundational layers of this amazing process of discovering your destiny in Christ.

Even if your history is riddled with bad things that God did not intend for you to experience, such as parents who made big mistakes, God can re-parent you. Ephesians 2:18–19 tells us, "For through Him we both have access by one Spirit to the Father. Now, therefore, you are no longer strangers and foreigners, but fellow citizens with the saints and members of the household of God."

Once you were born again, you entered the family of God; you are now a member of His household for eternity.

Like Joseph, as you forgive those who have hurt you in the past and embrace God's perspective on your pain, you can move forward to redeem the dreams of the past and see them fulfilled in your future.

FOUR
Designed for Significance

When Agnes Wells shared the interpretation of the voice I heard that night and prayed for me, it seemed clear that God had called me, for the time being, to be a worship leader.

Because of my reluctance, God supplied a powerful confirmation. The night after I heard the voice, Arthur Wells, the Old Guy's brother who had also seen Jesus in the bar that day, came to me and said, "The Lord spoke to me last night and told me to take you along with me on a revival tour, and God wants you to lead praise and worship for these meetings."

Although I didn't end up traveling with Arthur, I did begin leading worship on the reservation and in other contexts, and I continued to lead for the next twenty years. Worship leading was my first real ministry and the first stage of my life-long destiny. In order to understand the significance of this call to worship, it may help to look at another piece of my early life.

I was not raised in a musical home, but my father, Vincent Brodeur, was an accomplished artist. He graduated from the Chicago Art Institute and began his career drawing caricatures of tipsy tourists at various amusement parks around the nation. When we moved to San Francisco in 1960, my dad began to establish himself as a portrait artist in the city. Although he did well, he was unable to translate his success into money and ultimately had to become a commercial artist to pay the bills.

When I was a young child, my dad tried to involve me in artistic expression of various kinds. He spent hours training me how to draw and paint, but after a few years, it became obvious that I didn't have an artistic bone in my body. My dad was horribly disappointed that his number one son was such a failure, yet nothing could be done. It wasn't part of my design.

After this, my dad enrolled my sister and me in a private school that was established to support a serious ballet company. My sister was a prodigy, but again, I was a disappointment. I could not learn the moves or remember the steps, and I sabotaged every performance I was in. I quickly learned that being a world-class ballet dancer was also not part of my design.

But when I was fourteen years old, my dad bought me a guitar and a year of lessons, and everything in my life began to change. I finally found something I could do well. I discovered a dimension of my design. I studied classical, jazz, and ended up playing rock and roll. I organized different bands and played a number of small venues. By the time I finally gave my life to Jesus, the foundation was laid for my first stage of ministry: worship leading.

Design and Destiny

In this chapter, I want to turn our attention from the circumstances that shaped us in life to the deeper question of design. We have seen how God is in control of our histories and is able to redeem and restore even the most difficult circumstances for His purposes. In this chapter, I want to show how God is even in control of the way we are designed; our DNA, the color of our hair and eyes, and our natural abilities and talents were all hardwired into our original design at the moment of conception.

Fearfully and Wonderfully Made by God

The Lord knows you more intimately than you know yourself. He was present as you were formed in your mother's womb; He was there as your chromosomes developed and mitosis occurred. From conception to delivery, God was in the middle of every process that led to your existence.

Those of us who had a hard family life might be asking, "If God knows me and loved me, why did He put me in such a dysfunctional family?" Although the answer to this question has many facets and dimensions, it is helpful to remember that we live in a fallen world. God delegated authority to Adam and Eve, and when they gave up that authority to the devil, the consequences of their sin set in motion a whole series of events that is still impacting the world today. But this does not mean that you are bound by these consequences. On the contrary, you have come into relationship with the living God, the Creator of all things and the One who re-creates all things according to the counsel of His own will. You were not a surprise to God or an afterthought in His plan. You *are* His plan.

In the Sermon on the Mount, Jesus goes out of His way to describe the specific and intimate attention that

God pays to lilies and sparrows and even to the number of hairs on the human head. This caring attention did not begin when you became a believer—it began the moment you were conceived.

King David puts it this way in Psalm 139:13-16:

> You formed my inward parts;
> You covered me in my mother's womb.
> I will praise You, for I am fearfully [and] wonderfully made;
> Marvelous are Your works,
> And [that] my soul knows very well.
> My frame was not hidden from You,
> When I was made in secret,
> [And] skillfully wrought in the lowest parts of the earth.
> Your eyes saw my substance, being yet unformed.
> And in Your book they all were written,
> The days fashioned for me,
> When [as yet there were] none of them.

You and I are fearfully and wonderfully made. It may be hard for us to comprehend the degree to which God was personally involved in the formation of our being, but according to this psalm, God's involvement was absolute. Scripture makes it clear that God has intimate knowledge of every aspect of our being, and therefore, the very combination of the genetic factors that make us who we are is not outside of God's purview.

Verse 15 of Psalm 139 reveals that God knits us together in the core of our being, and He fashions us according to His unique design and purpose. He draws the DNA strands from mothers and fathers and combines them in the right order to provide the nature that He has ordained for us. This being true, it shouldn't surprise us that the unique combination of chromosomes that determines our design is perfectly aligned to the calling and destiny of the Lord in our lives.

It is wonderful to see how the Psalmist joins these two ideas of design and destiny together in the same paragraph: "Your eyes saw my substance, being yet unformed. And in Your book they all were written, the days fashioned for me, when as yet there were none of them" (Psalm 139:16). So in God's book, His database, everything that could be written down was written down. God records my design, and then He declares my destiny. God has determined that *who I am* is one of the strongest indicators of *who I will become*.

Design and Destiny Versus Free Will

As we explore the topic of divine design, we should take a moment to look at a big question: What about free will? Does God pre-determine and predestine everything? Is God the eternal scriptwriter who forces His actors to speak and act in absolute conformity to the play? The obvious answer is "No," but the question demands a deeper response. I don't believe that God sat down at the beginning of time, pre-programmed everything, and then watched us fall into a predicted pattern of predestined response.

Theologians and philosophers have argued for centuries about the apparent conflict between human free will and God's sovereign will. From my perspective, this conflict is merely a "false dichotomy" and misses the main point altogether. In my opinion, the answer to this age-old conflict is not found in either extreme but only in the relationship of time to eternity.

From Here to Eternity

God is an eternal Being who exists *outside of time*. Time and space were made by God to be a framework for the world in which we exist. God made human beings to live in time, *but He exists outside of time and interacts with all time at the same time* because He is eternal. Because of this, God is able to allow a limited amount of human free will while still maintaining His sovereign control.

One way to understand this concept is to picture a pianist sitting at the keys of a concert grand piano. Although the keys are placed in a chromatic order, the pianist is not bound by the ebony and ivory. The musician sits above the sequence of the keys and is free to play any key on the board at any time. In fact, this is what creates the true beauty of music and provides the chords and melodies that capture our hearts.

The sequence of time is like these keys on the piano. The keys exist in a clear order and sequence, but God sits above the piano and He can play whatever "notes" He chooses in whatever sequence He chooses, according to His own melody and His own composition. As I said before, God is outside of time and therefore can interact with every point in time at the same time.

God sees you at this very moment reading this page, but at this same moment (in *His* time), He sees you in your mother's womb. At this same moment, He can see you on your deathbed, and simultaneously, He can also see you a thousand years from now feasting with Him in the Heavens. Time binds us, but it does not bind God.

This perspective of time and eternity gives us the ability to affirm human free will *and* God's sovereign will at the same moment. God has invited us to play a duet with Him. Even when we play imperfectly or perhaps defiantly, He can override the notes we play and work all things together for good because He maintains final control of the musical performance.

Before the Foundations of the World

The Scriptures say that we were chosen in Him before the foundations of the world (Ephesians 1:4). How did that happen? How could we be chosen if we didn't yet exist? How could that verse be true if God were confined to time? The only possible answer is that God exists outside the foundations of the world, and the act of choosing us in time and space was done from an eternal position outside of time. Revelation 3:18 refers to Jesus as the "Lamb that was slain from the foundation of the world" because the act of the crucifixion — the sacrifice of Jesus on the Cross, the bearing of the sins of humanity — was an eternal act; it took place two thousand years ago in time and space, but the impact of that act was so eternal in its nature that it actually took place outside of time as well.

As a result of God's interaction with all time at the same time, He is able to work all things together for good without overriding our ability to choose. Ultimately, God does not want slaves who serve in blind obedience; He wants friends who will become full partners in His purposes. The only way this can happen is if our freedom to choose remains intact.

Before time began, the Author of time saw our unformed substance. He looked at us as we were developing, and He established destiny for us. God's mind is so vast, His database so comprehensive and inclusive, that He can micromanage every aspect of His Kingdom.

God's Choices and Our Choices

Because God affirms our power to choose, it is possible for us to make unwise decisions and "miss" the wonderful things that God designed us to do. There have been several times in my life when I made choices that were contrary to the will of God, and I took a "destiny detour." Yet God is so good that even when we err and choose to step off the path He has laid out for us, He intervenes and continually steers us toward the fulfillment of who we are called to be.

> How precious also are Your thoughts to me, O God!
> How great is the sum of them!
> If I should count them, they would be more in number than the sand;
> When I awake, I am still with You (Psalm 139:17–18).

I like to think of God's will as an interstate freeway. God is moving us from a state of immaturity to a state of fruitfulness and fulfillment in Jesus. God wants to move us into the fast lane where our journey can be free from hindrances and distractions. However, every so often, we become enamored with the attractions by the side of the road, and we choose the off-ramp. It doesn't really matter what motivated us to do so; whether hunger, thirst, pride, fear, or any other temptation, we find ourselves on the side streets of God's will. But again, God is so good that even when we make poor choices, He always creates new on-ramps to the freeway of destiny in our lives. His purpose is to fulfill us as we fulfill Him. "I know the plans I have for you," He says, "the thoughts I have toward you, thoughts to do you good" (Jeremiah 29:11).

God has ordained certain good works for us to accomplish, which were prepared for us from the foundations of the world (Ephesians 2:10). We might make mistakes along the way, but we call Him the God of the second chance, and He always turns the second chance into the first chance. By God's grace, Plan B becomes Plan A, and the mystery of redemption is displayed once again. We can see numerous examples in Scripture in which individuals made choices that sabotaged their destinies, but as they returned to the Lord, He eventually returned to them.

Nature Versus Nurture

Another important controversy emerges when we begin to discuss the topic of God's design, and it centers on the question of nature versus nurture. Some people hold that our biological makeup has very little affect on our potential as individuals. These people believe that we are almost entirely a product of our environment. On the other hand, there are those who believe that the potential of an individual is almost entirely determined by his or her lineage and genetic makeup. But recent genetic research is now showing that genetic factors are not as absolute as once thought. This series of amazing studies began with a look at identical twins in an attempt to understand why those who were born with the exact same genome could develop a different genetic disease. The evidence revealed another set of factors that influence the human genome: the *epigenome*. The epigenome works like an electrical switch that turns on or off certain genetic factors within an individual depending on environmental factors. These factors include scarcity, abundance, love, abuse, and a wide variety of other influences. These scientists suggested that maternal love (nurture) could turn on or off certain genes and keep them from functioning. Environmental factors such as famine, severe drought, or trauma can also turn on or off the epigenome.

What do these findings show us? We are creatures of both design and environmental impact—of nature *and* nurture. God is aware of these factors and how they compose the character and personality development of a child. The good news is that God is able to work in the life of a person with genetic challenges and bring forth a great destiny, and He is also able to work in someone with great genetic design and influence him or her to be even greater.

Character and personality strengths are key components in our ability to *fulfill* our destinies. On the other hand, character and personality weaknesses are the primary cause of unfulfilled destiny. Personality is mostly a factor of nature, while character is largely a result of nurture. As important as both these factors are, it is also important to remember that God is bigger than genetics and He is greater than environments, and He is able to do exceedingly above all we ask or think. And He is able to work within us to will and to do of His good pleasure.

Family Is the Foundation

Just as God is the author of our "nature," He is also the overseer of our "nurture." Although the Lord largely determines our design, our families shape our destinies. Family is the foundation of personal destiny. God established the family as the source of identity and the transmitter of destiny. The calling of every individual is incubated in the family from generation to generation. This is why healthy families are so absolutely essential to a healthy world.

In the very beginning, God set in motion the structure of a family: a father, a mother, and their children. This family creates community that ideally establishes God's purposes in the heart of a child.

Unfortunately, because of sin, broken parents raised broken children, who became the next generation of broken parents, ultimately impacting every corner of the earth. One of the goals of Christian families is to reverse the trend of generational brokenness and to have *blessings* flow through our bloodlines rather than curses. This is why the restoration and preservation of the family is at the heart of every revival and transformational effort.

Even though most of the Western Church has been built upon a pro-family foundation, as a pastor I have seen many parents who did not understand or appreciate the family that God had given them. In some cases, the misuse of Scripture led to the abuse of children. It is time for mothers and fathers throughout the land to embrace their pivotal role as the founders of the next generation. Psalm 127:3 gives us the purpose, the *design*, of family: "Behold, children are a heritage from the LORD, the fruit of the womb is a reward." Clearly, God's perspective is that children are our true treasure. Some of our culture has fallen into a grave misconception, believing that children are nuisances or that they are beings to raise and get out of the house so we can get on with our careers or retirement years.

Children are our heritage, but they are also our legacy. The psalm continues in verses 4-5:

> Like arrows in the hand of a warrior,
> So are the children of one's youth.
> Happy is the man who has his quiver full of them;
> They shall not be ashamed,
> But shall speak with their enemies in the gate.

What does the image of the quiver imply? This is an archery analogy that encourages us to take out our arrows, put them in our bows, aim them in the right direction, and let them fly. That is how a dad and a mom are supposed to direct their children—with the intention and precision of an archer.

Many of us were never "aimed" by our parents. Many of our parents never called forth the destiny inside of us. One of the main "jobs" of parents is to identify, celebrate, and bring forth the gifts and callings of their children. If parents do not fulfill their role, their children often become part of an aimless generation, like arrows shot without a target.

The job of parenting is of the highest importance, and that is why it is the focus of constant attack. Many of us come from shattered families, torn by divorce, and unfortunately, divorce rips at the core of a child's confidence and identity. A broken family often inflicts a child with instability, grief, anger, fear, insecurity, and other harmful things that can later become sabotage points on the path to the fulfillment of personal destiny.

In Jesus, we have been brought into a new family, and if we can enter into the full understanding of the spirit of adoption that is outlined in Romans 8:14-15, we can receive the spirit of sonship, be healed of the wounds of orphanhood in our lives, and begin to see the restoration of the foundations that we are missing because of the brokenness of our homes and families of origin.

We Are People of Choice

The final area I want to explore as we look at the subject of God's design is the area of personal choices. Our design is something beyond our choice, a factor of circumstances beyond our control. But our design is foundational to what we choose and how we choose later in life.

Personal choices—what you choose to believe and do about the world, God, yourself, and others—can either make or break destiny fulfillment in your life. The things that you say about yourself, others, and God will anchor those beliefs in your heart. In other words, the choices you make on the basis of what you believe and agree with will become determinative factors in your life.

When we believe and say negative things about ourselves and think that we don't have what it takes to succeed in life, we actually disempower ourselves in respect to our destinies. When we doubt that God will provide for our needs, we inadvertently work against God's provision in our lives. When we question God's commitment to defend and protect us, we set ourselves up for greater vulnerability. What we choose to believe directly affects what we receive. It is vital that we train ourselves to think only what God thinks and to say what God says. From this foundation, we are empowered to do what God does.

In a later chapter, we will be discussing strongholds of the mind: "houses" or patterns of thought that do not reflect God's truth. In many cases, we are not aware that our thoughts and perspectives do not align with Scripture, which is why we actively need to "bring every thought into captivity to the obedience of Christ" (2 Corinthians 10:5). When our thoughts are held in obedience to Christ, we will find much greater freedom in our lives.

We Are Unique

In summary, let's agree that each of us is uniquely *gifted* and *specifically designed* by God. In His sovereignty, He oversaw the moment of our conception and the unique combination of genetic factors that have determined our "nature." He ordained the family to be the foundation of each civilization—the "riverbanks" for guiding children forward into their individual destinies. However, through sin, the human family became infected and became a primary conduit of pain and brokenness. Broken parents tend to produce broken children, and even the healthiest family can carry the wounds produced by sin.

In Jesus, we have been brought into a new family. Through Him, we can receive the spirit of sonship, be healed of the wounds of orphanhood in our lives, and begin to see the restoration of the foundations that we are missing because of the brokenness of our homes and families of origin.

Jesus continually steers us toward the fulfillment of our destiny. Even if we make mistakes along the way, God always creates new on-ramps to the freeway of destiny in our lives. His purpose is to fulfill us as we fulfill Him. So even though we may experience hardship, we do not have to be afraid of missing what He has for us, because He is fully capable of working *all* things for our good.

FIVE

Introducing the Discovery Process

After my time in Montana, I returned to northern California with a solid foundation in my newfound faith. I knew I needed to continue to grow, so I began to look at various training opportunities. At the same time, I began to feel a strong calling back to San Francisco, and a friend told me about a ministry called Gospel Outreach that provided on-the-job training for aspiring ministers. They were also planning to plant a new church in San Francisco. It was clearly God's will for me, and after six months of training at the Lighthouse Ranch, I moved to the city to help establish a new church. It was the fall of 1977.

Two years after moving back to San Francisco, I met an amazing man named Paul Pillai. Paul was from India and was traveling by bus from city to city raising money for his ministry in his homeland. I picked him up at the bus station and brought him to our "ministry house," where we were taking in around twenty people off the street every night. We hosted around forty different people every week, providing them with a hot meal, a warm bed, and a nightly Bible study in our cramped little living room.

We were excited to have our special guest share his personal story with the group. That night, a new unmarried couple had come off the streets to spend the evening with us. After Paul shared about his ministry in India, he invited people to receive Christ, and this couple raised their hands. After praying with them, he asked them to write out their names so he could pray for them during the next few weeks. As they wrote down their names, Paul's eyes got really big. He went over to his briefcase and took out a piece of paper with their names on it. He said, "Three months ago, the Lord gave me your names to pray for, and I have been praying for you both—from India!"

That got my attention. I hadn't seen this level of supernatural expression since I was in Montana. The next morning, Paul took me aside and told me that the Lord had spoken to him on the previous night about me and about my calling.

He then began to tell me what God had shared with him about my destiny. He said my calling would unfold in stages and that I was first called to do the work of an evangelist, then a pastor, and eventually I would be called to an apostolic ministry where I would oversee churches and work in the broader Body of Christ coaching and pastoring pastors. He also said that I would be used by God to heal the sick, cast out demons, and impact nations.

I was floored. I was just twenty-two years old at the time and barely out of spiritual diapers. Although I had always suspected that I had a high calling on my life, this news came as a shock to me. I didn't know if I was ready, and I knew for sure that I wasn't worthy. I couldn't imagine how God was going to bring all this to pass.

Within a few months, I had co-founded a new ministry called SOS San Francisco, and I spent the next seven years preaching the Gospel on the streets of our city and leading others to do so as well. In 1984, after years of intensive training, my wife and I pioneered a church that we ended up pastoring for the next twenty-five years. In more recent years, I have moved into an apostolic leadership role where I am serving in multiple ministries to create greater effectiveness and impact in the wider Body of Christ. By the grace of God, each aspect of Paul Pillai's prophecy has come to pass. We did our part and responded in obedience to divine summons, and God did His part and brought my destiny into reality. I look forward to the future as God's purpose continues to unfold.

The Three Dimensions of Spiritual Gifts

How about you? You may not have received a personal prophecy or a voice from Heaven about your destiny, but there is absolutely no doubt that God has called you to serve Him in specific ways. Knowing this, the next step is to begin the discovery process and identify your spiritual gifts, your Kingdom passions, and the specific spheres to which you are called.

This chapter provides an introduction to the discovery process and outlines the various spiritual gifts that are presented in Scripture. We will see that there are three primary categories, or three dimensions, of spiritual gifts, each of which provides a distinct dimension of our spiritual identity. Just as there are three dimensions in basic geometry, these three dimensions of gifting define the height, width, and depth of our spiritual impact. These gifts also provide the innate abilities that empower us to fulfill our responsibilities in life, work, and ministry.

Before we continue, I would like to give a quick disclaimer: *We should always be careful when forming categories from Scripture.* Various lists are given in the Bible to help us grow in our understanding and application of truth. These lists are not necessarily comprehensive or conclusive, and they are not meant to be boxes to limit God or to limit us. On the contrary, they are given to empower us to fulfill everything that God has called us to do.

The three categories of gifts upon which we will focus are sometimes called ministry gifts, the motivational gifts, and the manifestation gifts. In this chapter, I will give a brief overview of each set of gifts and also present a few other dimensions of calling that can help you as you begin to discover your destiny in the Lord.

The Ascension or Ministry Gifts: *Ephesians 4:11–12*

> And He gave some [to be] apostles, prophets, evangelists, pastors and teachers; to equip the saints for the work of the ministry for the building up of the Body of Christ (Ephesians 4:11–12).

These spiritual gifts are often called the "office gifts" and refer to the way that we serve and minister to one another in the Body of Christ and to the world beyond. I refer to these as the ascension gifts because they were given at the time when Jesus ascended into Heaven. We are told that "when He ascended on high, He led captivity captive and gave gifts to men."

That statement is an extension of Ephesians 3:10, which says, "to the intent that now the manifold wisdom of God might be made known... by the church." In other words, when Jesus ascended, He poured out His gifts into His Church so that we could display His wisdom throughout the earth.

It is important to remember that all of these ascension gifts — *apostle, prophet, evangelist, pastor,* and *teacher* – are aspects of the ministry of Jesus. He was known as the apostle and high priest of our faith, the great prophet, the good shepherd and teacher, and He was the One who brought the Good News as the premier evangelist of our faith. On earth, Jesus *was* all of these gifts, and He gave these gifts to His Body, so that we would not only reflect His character but also His capabilities. Yet He did not give every single member every one of His gifts; rather, He gave each of us a piece, or portion, of Himself so that we would need one another to display Him fully.

Think about it like this: Jesus is the white light that shines into the "prism" of the Church and refracts into a rainbow of different colors. Each one of these colors is a manifestation of His ministry. When Paul writes that Christ gave gifts to men, he is quoting Psalm 68:18, which includes even the rebellious as recipients of the gifts; therefore, I believe that a case can be made that the ascension gifts were given to all humanity, even to those who do not yet know the Lord. In other words, God poured out His Spirit on *all* flesh, and *everyone* has these gifts wired into his or her inner being.

If you look carefully, it is possible to identify secular apostles, secular prophets, secular teachers, and others who don't know Jesus but are still functioning in some expression of His ministry because these gifts were poured out on all flesh. These gifts are part of each person's unique design, but these gifts cannot function in their full glory until our hearts are fully submitted to God. When He comes into our lives and we begin to walk in the callings that God has given us, we can then begin to walk in the fullness of His gifts for His glory.

As a side note, I don't think that the ascension gifts were given as strict categories. I have had the privilege of knowing and walking closely with at least a half dozen apostolic leaders, and not one of them was the same as another. They all had different colors in the prism—colors that were obviously influenced by other aspects of their uniqueness, such as their childhoods, personal choices, or their other ministry gifts.

So I believe that these gifts express themselves in hybrid form. There are apostolic prophets who are distinct from prophetic apostles—or a pastoral teacher and an evangelistic teacher. There are different colors and combinations among the gifts that affect how a person operates them. The very combination makes each leader distinct.

Unfortunately, some have misused these gifts by focusing on position and titles rather than service and function. In so doing, these individuals have given these ministry gifts a bad name and have caused many people to be offended. I am looking forward to emerging leaders embracing these gifts in a way that gives glory to God rather than glory to the leader.

The Motivational Gifts: *Romans 12:3-8*

The gifts found in Romans 12:3-8 have historically been called "motivational" gifts and tend to define the personality or the "way" in which we interact with one another. This term was originally coined by Bill Gothard, the founder of Institutes in Basic Youth Conflicts, but has since been adopted by many other leaders. In this passage, Paul describes the Church as a body with many different parts. Although each part functions differently, they are all dependent on one another for the body to be whole. There are seven motivational gifts: the prophet, minister, teacher, exhorter, giver, leader, and comforter. Each of these gifts describes the style and the *flavor* of our individual ministries.

Why would it be important for each person to have a different *flavor* in his or her ministry style? As we talked about earlier, we each have a different "light" or "color" of God that we present to the world. In Ephesians 3, Paul says his calling is to declare the "unfathomable riches of Christ" so that the "manifold wisdom of God might now be made known." That is just one reason that each of us is different — because God's wisdom is "manifold." We could never reflect all of who He is.

The Spiritual Gifts: *1 Corinthians 12:4–14*

Paul begins 1 Corinthians 12 by saying, "Now concerning spiritual gifts, brethren, I do not want you to be ignorant." It is interesting to note that in the original Greek text, the word *gift* never occurs. It is the word *pneuma*, and its clearest literal translation would be "spiritual things" or "spirituals." So the verse could read, "Now concerning *spirituals*, brethren, I do not want you to be ignorant."

This passage is the text we normally use when we refer to spiritual gifts. However, if you look at the context of this passage, it actually begins back in 1 Corinthians

11:33, which says, "Therefore, my brethren, when you come together..." Paul then goes on to talk about communion and other aspects of their gatherings. Then he calls their attention to the supernatural expressions that were happening among them. Paul was concerned about the fact that there was much competition and disunity in their expression of the gifts. In response to this, Paul underscores that there may be different gifts, but there is only *one* Spirit.

Next, Paul goes through the list of nine gifts: the word of wisdom, word of knowledge, gift of faith, gift of healings, working of miracles, prophecy, discerning of spirits, gift of tongues, and interpretation of tongues. Each of these gifts has a tremendous power that I will expound upon later.

It is my conviction that if you have the Holy Spirit living in you, you have access to all the gifts of the Spirit. I believe that every believer can function in any of these gifts as the Spirit wills; however, because of your unique design, you will tend to operate in one or two of these gifts more fluently than the others.

Passion and Dreams

As we have discussed, your uniqueness is a combination of your design, your choices, your beliefs, and your spiritual gifts. Another element that contributes to your uniqueness is your sense of Kingdom passion and dream.

What moves you deep in your heart? What problems in the world trouble you? What causes do you care about? What do you really want to do with your life? What would you do if you had no limitations and knew you couldn't fail? Each of these questions is designed to help you identify your God-given passions and dreams.

We will be talking more about the way in which passions and dreams can interact with destiny in a later chapter, but I want to mention them here because they are connected to the gifts and calling that God has given us. Passion and dream have significant roles in the formation and understanding of personal destiny.

Scope of Ministry

Along with this combination of design, gifts, and passion, every person also has a unique *scope* of ministry. Some of us will function most effectively on a one-on-one basis, some in a small group, some in a mid-sized community, and others in a larger congregation. Some of us are called to function internationally or as itinerant ministers, while others are called to function right next door.

In Exodus 18, Moses and his father-in-law, Jethro, discussed how Moses was wearing himself thin by trying to serve all of the people. Jethro proposed that Moses delegate to others and find different men who could minister to tens and fifties and hundreds and thousands. Moses followed his advice and better served his people.

Paul puts it this way in 2 Timothy 2:2: "And the things that you have heard from me among many witnesses, commit these to faithful men who will be able to teach others also." Each of us has a scope of ministry that the Lord has given us. Some of us will lead a few people; some of us will lead many people. One scope is not more important than another—it all revolves around the special, unique function to which God has called us.

Sphere of Ministry

Finally, another distinction that makes you unique in your calling and destiny is the *sphere* to which you are called. There are many different spheres in society, and you and I are called to impact and influence these spheres as part of the Great Commission. I have identified five primary spheres of society: family, culture, economy, government, and faith. Within these five primary spheres, there are dozens of other secondary spheres in which God also desires to be represented.

Every believer is called to be a minister, but not all ministers are called to minister in a church. In fact, the majority of people will find their primary ministry outside of a church building. You may be a children's church worker, usher, or worship leader on a Sunday morning, but what are you doing the rest of the week? If you are like most people, you probably have an occupation or profession in which you spend your time and talents. You may be a stay-at-home mom or a barista at a coffee shop. You may be a movie producer, an athlete, a soldier, or a CEO of a corporation. No matter what you do in your life, you are first and foremost a minister of God's Kingdom. You are still that unique person with a unique design, functioning in your occupation with the heart of a servant and the heart of a leader. God wants to make your occupation your vocation.

God's purpose for you is that you would bring the Kingdom wherever you go. You can bring the Kingdom in a Starbucks, as a professor in a college, or as a commercial pilot in the skies. You are called to minister within the context of the life in which you live—that is where all ministry is supposed to take place. Which sphere are you called to? What people group do you feel drawn to pray for? Who are the people you are called to serve? How can you extend God's loving Kingdom into the sphere in which you are called?

Ultimately, God's purpose in Christ Jesus is to restore all things to Himself, and He has positioned believers in every sphere of society—people who are motivated by their callings in Christ—in order that His redemptive work occurs.

How to Open Your Gifts

As you prepare to walk in your unique gifts and ministries, there are five steps you can take to begin to "open up" the full destiny God has for you.

Before we look at these steps, however, it is important to remember that every gift proceeds from the Giver, and every calling comes from the One who calls. God loves you so much that He sent His Son to die for you. If God loves you, you ought to love yourself.

God sees you as loveable and valuable, and you need to embrace *God's* attitude toward you and begin to understand that you are great—not in some proud, self-serving sense, but in the sense that you are awesome in God because God has made you to be an awesome being.

Get to Know Yourself in the Lord

The first step in the discovery process is to invite the

Lord to show you *who you really are*. You are amazing, and you are called to be amazing. Get to know yourself in Christ, and then begin to approximate the purpose of your history. Look back through your life and see the trajectory—the line of guidance that the Lord has brought you along. Look at where you are compared to where you were; connect the dots, find a line, get on the other side of it, do a one-eighty, and look forward. Where does that line continue?

What is the purpose of your personal and spiritual history, and how does it pertain to your destiny? God doesn't need to start with a perfect person in order to fashion a perfect destiny. See your history as He sees your history. Lay down every regret and begin to celebrate the ways in which God has woven all the threads of your life into the phenomenal tapestry that carries your image. Let Him show you who you really are: an amazing man or woman of God with amazing potential.

Forgive Yourself and Others

Another step in the discovery process is to embrace a life of forgiveness. You need to forgive everyone who has harmed you, and you also need to forgive yourself. Many times, we hold our true selves at a distance because we are ashamed of the things we have done and the things we have left undone. Although most of us have a firm belief that Jesus died for our sins, our belief in His forgiveness doesn't translate into an ability to forgive ourselves. We must totally and completely forgive and release ourselves from everything that keeps us bound, and only then will we be free to discover our true destiny without limitations.

It may sound humanistic, but if Jesus forgave you, you

cannot hold anything against yourself; the blood that was shed two thousand years ago on the Cross of Calvary was shed for *all* sin. As it says in Hebrews 10, the purpose of that blood being shed was to cleanse our consciences from every dead work to serve the living God. So it is essential that we apply that blood completely to others and to ourselves and release our consciences from anything that may bind us to the past.

Embrace Your Call

The third step in the discovery process is to take responsibility for your life and embrace the uniqueness of the call of God that is at work in you. In spite of all our limitations and hindrances, God has worked all things together for good up to this point, and He will continue to do the same into the future.

It is time for us to set aside blame and excuses. It is time to move beyond fear and anxiety and step boldly into the ministry that God has given you. Start where you are and do what you can. See a need and do your best to humbly fill it. If you are faithful in little things, God will make you a leader over many things. Stop disqualifying yourself because God is the One who has qualified you.

As you step into serving others in immediate ways, God will work within you to prepare you for ultimate things. Don't let the fear of failure hinder you any longer—it is time to embrace the call of God.

Identify Your Spiritual Passions

The fourth step in the discovery process is to pay close attention to the things that attract you and the things that repulse you: Get to know your likes and dislikes. As a pastoral life coach, I have worked with people who were unable to identify a sense of *dream* in their lives. Then I started asking them what they did not like about the church, themselves, or the people around them. In finding what they disliked, I could often get a clear idea of the Kingdom dream they were created to realize.

As you get to know others in Christ, you will discover the gifts within them that attract you. Think about the people in Scripture or in history who are your heroes. You perceive them as such because they reflect an aspect of your destiny. As you identify your heroes, the question you need to focus on is not *who* but *why*. For instance, what about King David makes me attracted to his story? Why am I attracted to Paul, Esther, or Deborah? It is because these people reflect aspects of my calling.

Who are the leaders you have admired or desired to follow? Who are the heroes in your own life? All of the traits that attract you to these people are reflections of your deepest desires and your sense of destiny.

Get Connected to Others

The final discovery step that we will discuss here is the priority of connection. You and I were created for community, and we ultimately cannot know ourselves fully apart from relationships. Your gifts and calling are confirmed in the community of believers.

One way to get to know our destiny in community is

by observing the fruit we bear the most in others. When I am with people, how do they respond? What comes alive inside of them as a result of who I am? When I understand these things and begin to see the impact I have in other people's lives, I start to understand myself more fully.

On the other hand, if I try to force myself into certain activities with others and it doesn't bear good fruit, I can conclude that I am probably not gifted in that area. However, when people respond positively in my presence and I know why, I can get an idea of who I am called to be.

These five steps of discovery are a great starting point for your journey. As you engage in this process, you will learn more about yourself, as well as have more confidence about what you are called to do and who you are called to be in the Lord.

In the next chapters, we will begin to look more closely at the specific gifts that God has given to us and discover how they work in our lives. As a result, you will see how generously God has given of Himself to empower you to fulfill His purpose on the earth.

SIX
Your Destiny Orientation

In his second letter to the churches, the apostle Peter exhorts us to make our calling and our election sure. This verse has impacted my personal life in a dramatic way.

About six months after my wife, Diane, and I were married, we were sitting in our living room praying for direction from God. Diane received a clear, open vision of a man praying over us in a large room filled with many people. Then she heard a Scripture: "Your calling and election will be made sure."

We didn't know what this vision meant, so we filed it away for a later time. About three weeks later, we were called by our denominational organization to attend a pastors' gathering in Santa Cruz, California. At the time, we were still studying for our ordination, so it was unusual that they would invite us to a gathering of this kind. We figured that it must be God's will, so we said, "Yes," and signed up for the conference. When we arrived at the conference center, we walked into the main assembly area. Diane grabbed me by the arm and said, "Michael, this is the room I saw in that vision." Needless to say, we were surprised. A little later, as the room began to fill with people, she said, "Yes, this is definitely the room, but the person who was praying for us in the vision is not here."

Three days later, the final keynote speaker arrived. His name was Erskine Holt, and he had been a significant figure in the revivals of the last century. When my wife saw him, she said, "That's the man who was praying for us!" This series of events amazed and excited us, but there was a major problem: It would be impossible for him to pray for us because we were not ordained and didn't have the proper level of seniority.

But two days later, as Holt was ordaining those who were called to be evangelists, one of the recently ordained prophetic leaders came to me and said, "You need to go up and get prayer."

I tried to explain to him that our going forward to receive prayer would be perceived by everyone in the room as a breach in protocol, but he just grabbed us by the arms and dragged us to the front.

It took quite a bit of time for him to come down the line, praying for people. When he got to us and laid hands on our heads, he stopped praying and said, "You're not called to be evangelists. You have a different calling." He began to pronounce over us the same destiny that the Lord had already spoken through Paul Pillai, whom I mentioned in the last chapter. It was a profound point of input that solidified many things for us.

This encounter confirmed God's purposes and made our calling and election very sure. The Scriptures tell us "by the mouth of two or three shall every word be confirmed," and we felt so strongly that God had confirmed His calling in our lives.

The Ministry Gifts

Beginning in the preface, we looked at how the Book of Ephesians establishes within us a sense of identity. It tells us who we are in Christ: accepted, beloved, and chosen by God from the foundations of the world. Toward the end of the first chapter, Paul prays that the Church "may know what is the hope of His calling, what are the riches of the glory of His inheritance in the saints" (Ephesians 1:18).

Paul continues by talking about how we were children of wrath in times past (because of the Fall), but then God, who is rich in mercy, loved us, saved us, and gave each of us a calling: "For we are His workmanship, created in Christ Jesus for good works" (Ephesians 2:10). As we talked about before, those "good works" are not simply everyday good deeds we do for our families and the people around us; they are the steps of destiny and calling—they are what each of us was created by God to do in life.

Paul goes on to explain that we are no longer strangers or foreigners, held separate from God's family, but all of us are being built together into a single house, a dwelling place of God in the Spirit, with a foundation of the apostles and prophets. In chapter 3, we hear about the manifold (multicolored) wisdom of God, and then chapter 4 opens with a call to humility just before introducing this next set of gifts.

This brings us to Paul's list of the ascension, or ministry, gifts, which we briefly looked at in the last chapter. Paul explains here that when Christ ascended on high, He gave gifts to men:

> And He Himself gave some [to be] **apostles**, some **prophets**, some **evangelists**, and some **pastors** and **teachers**, for the equipping of the saints for the work of ministry, for the edifying of the body of Christ, till we all come to the unity of the faith and of the knowledge of the Son of God, to a perfect man, to the measure of the stature of the fullness of Christ (Ephesians 4:11–13).

In this passage, Paul gives us a picture of what God's purposes are. We move from identity into authority, from authority into family, and from family into destiny.

Although some theologians may argue that these gifts are no longer for today, a simple look at the passage will challenge that perspective:

These gifts were given at the same time: at Jesus' ascension.

They were given for the same purpose: equipping the saints for the work of ministry.

They were given *until* the same time: until we perfectly express Jesus on the earth.

Unless I am mistaken, we have not yet come into the "unity of the faith and of the knowledge of the Son of God, to a perfect man, to the measure of the stature of the fullness of Christ." Therefore, these gifts must still be at work today to produce that result.

These gifts were poured out on all of humanity, and everyone has access to at least one of them. As we've discussed, many people usually do not have just a single gift but rather what we might call a gift-*mix*, which usually consists of a dominant gift with secondary gifts that add flavor and dimension. At the same time, it is important to remember that these gifts are not necessarily distributed in equal scope of impact. Some will minister at an interpersonal or small group level. These individuals may be functioning pastorally or prophetically, but it would be misleading to give them the title of "pastor" or "prophet" without a season of significant proving and the confirmation of widely recognized leaders of the same stature. Ordination to a ministry "office" is something that should be conducted only with great wisdom and counsel. Unfortunately, one of the reasons many have rejected these ministry gifts is that there are so many self-appointed apostles and prophets who have given the true expression a bad name. Sadly, the presence of the counterfeit has undermined the value of the real thing.

Still, it is God who has invested these gifts in individuals, and these individuals are called to express these gifts in some form of leadership, impacting and influencing those around them. So, if you are called to serve as an apostle, the primary function of your apostolic ministry is not only to do the work of an apostle, but it is also to equip others to be apostolic. The same applies if you are a prophet; your purpose isn't only to prophesy—it is actually to equip others to prophesy. If you're a pastor, your purpose is not just to care for the flock but also to train the members of the flock to care for one another.

Since all these gifts were given to equip believers, it is safe to assume that every individual believer is called to function in some dimension of the apostolic, prophetic, evangelistic, pastoral, and teaching. You are called to function in all these gifts as you are equipped. But according to your unique design, you will have a propensity to function more often and more effectively in one gift above the others.

Let us begin to look at each one of these ascension gifts in more detail.

The Apostolic Gift (Builder)

Mentoring and Mobilizing People for Ministry, Mission, and Multiplication

The word *apostle* means "a sent one." This doesn't mean a person with an errand. Rather, it means a person who has been sent with the full authority of the one who sends: a delegated representative or ambassador. In fact, because the apostolic gift is an imparting and equipping gift as well, it literally means "a sent one who sends." In other words, an apostle is a sent one, and as I begin to understand that my first responsibility is to impart the "sent" dynamic to others, I become a sent one who sends.

Traditionally, the Church has attached a lot of "mystical" meaning to the term "apostle," which has caused us to elevate the gift beyond the reach of the average individual. But actually in Scripture, there are over twenty-five different people listed as apostles and one of them was a woman. Contrast this with the fact that there is only one person in the New Testament who has the title of "pastor" and that is Jesus. The word *pastor* is used only one time as a noun when it didn't refer to Jesus, and that is in this amazing passage of Ephesians 4:11. Yet we now use the word *pastor* freely and avoid the word *apostle* because we have mistakenly believed the gift passed away in the first century. While it is true that the word *apostle* was used less and less after the Book of Acts, that does not mean the gift passed away.

The apostolic role is about two primary functions. The first is seeing the heavenly blueprint and bringing Heaven to earth. The second function consists of mentoring and mobilizing men and women for ministry, mission, and multiplication. Apostles help people understand their gift-mixes, get them moving in their actual giftings, and mentor them along the way. The apostolic purpose is the fulfillment of the greater purposes of God. Apostles look for people who can be activated right away to serve others.

Ministry means serving God and others. Apostolic leaders serve by identifying and developing emerging apostolic leaders, while at the same time helping everyone else fulfill their ministries as well. Apostles desire to see people mobilized according to their unique callings and gift-mixes so they can fulfill their missions in life. The apostolic mandate is to ensure that the mission of Jesus is being fulfilled in the members of the body, individually and corporately. Ultimately, the apostolic goal is to see the leaders who are being mobilized and mentored multiply themselves so that they are pouring out their lives into others and activating *them* into their gifts and callings, so that the Body of Christ reflects Jesus fully on the earth.

The apostle's function within churches and ministries is to serve as a spiritual father or mother, providing pioneering, oversight, and renewal. Apostolic leaders are wired to push beyond the boundaries of the status quo and advance God's Kingdom throughout the earth. They see the blueprints for building the house of God; they see what has been built in the past and keep it going, but they also look into the future to see what needs to be built next: people, organizations, churches, and so forth.

Paul gives us a great example of the apostolic ministry in 1 Corinthians 3:10–11:

> According to the grace of God which was given to me, as a wise master builder I have laid the foundation,

and another builds on it. But let each one take heed how he builds on it. For no other foundation can anyone lay than that which is laid, which is Jesus Christ.

In other words, he is saying, "I'm the general contractor who's seen the blueprint and who's hiring the subcontractors to get the work done. Everyone needs to come into this process in a way that honors the blueprint that I'm seeing."

Implicit in the apostolic gift is a heavenly vision. After relating his encounter with Jesus in Acts 26, Paul says, "Therefore, King Agrippa, I was not disobedient to the heavenly vision" (verse 19). An apostolic leader sees the vision of Jesus for His Church, not just the local churches, but also the Church at large—the Kingdom of God. He or she is able to see aspects and components of it that are unique and specific to the vision. I do not believe every apostle sees the exact same picture, but each sees the right picture for the sphere that he or she is called to serve in. Once the apostle has the picture in mind, he or she then translates it into a series of steps that brings it into the natural realm.

Apostles see the big picture and are able to break it down and assign pieces to the subcontractors. They are able to see where each of the gifts fits into the equation of God's purposes and mobilize people to work together in teams for the accomplishment of the task. There are strategic, tactical, and logistical dimensions to the apostolic ministry, so overall, apostles are builders.

In Scripture, we see various expressions of the apostolic gifting demonstrated. Take Paul and Peter for example. Paul, as a pioneering apostle, went where little or no foundation existed; he liked to build from scratch. He was a catalytic apostle and made circuits, going from place to place ordaining elders. Sometimes he stayed in a city for only a few days, but he left a church wherever he went. In addition to pioneering and building, Paul was a teaching apostle as well. He was very didactic and brought logic and structure to the Faith.

Peter, on the other hand, was more of a pastoral apostle. There is no record of Peter ever planting a church apart from the church in Jerusalem, which was actually planted by Jesus Himself. Peter was given the keys of the Kingdom, but he never went out to plant. Instead, he went out to provide oversight and renewal, and his main function was as a sending apostle. He generally stayed in one place and ministered from there.

We find different kinds of apostolic leaders in Scripture as well as in modern life, so in order to understand the individual destiny God has given each of us, we need to understand the differences and distinctions of this gifting. Remember that these are not strict categories. I currently know a prophetic apostle, an evangelistic apostle, and a pastoral apostle. There are different dimensions of the apostolic gifting that will combine to create the unique design that the Lord has placed inside of that person for the purpose he or she is called to fulfill.

As I stated earlier, I believe there are apostles outside the Church as well because as the psalmist indicates, these gifts were given to "even the rebellious, that He might dwell among them"(Psalm 68:18). Non-believing apostles function as leaders of leaders in high-level management; they are often pioneers, franchisers, or entrepreneurs.

What makes Joe's Coffee Shop on the corner different from Starbucks? There is an apostolic expression in the latter that has caused it to multiply around the world. That is an indicator of the apostolic gift.

Whether you are a Paul, a Peter, or the founder of a major corporation, the responsibility of an apostle is equipping, sending, and calling people to fulfill their highest purposes and potentials. They are pioneers and builders who cannot help but behold a Kingdom vision and give their lives to see God's people realize this reality.

The Prophetic Gift (Revealer)

Discerning and Declaring God's Power, Presence, and Perspective

The prophet is God's confidant and God's spokesperson. The Bible says that the prophetic gift functions in tandem with the apostolic ministry. The Church is built upon the foundation of the apostles and prophets — Jesus Christ Himself being the chief cornerstone (Ephesians 2:20). Scripture provides examples of the apostolic and prophetic functioning together in various ways. In Acts 15, Silas and Jude were sent out with Paul and Barnabas to confirm the word that came from the apostolic council in Jerusalem. Years later, a prophet named Agabus came to Paul, took off Paul's belt, and wrapped himself up in it. He said that the owner of that belt would be chained up and taken to Rome. And sure enough, Paul later found himself in chains. That was a prophetic act that also proved correct (Acts 21:8–11). There are many other examples of prophets functioning alongside the apostles as well.

The Greek word *prophetes* means "to speak forth the

anointed word of God." The implication is that prophets have spent time with God and that they know how to hear the voice of God – either through dreams and visions or the direct voice of God. Sometimes prophets hear God's audible voice, and sometimes they receive other kinds of impressions or insights that are an expression of their prophetic gift.

Part of the prophet's responsibility is to focus on discerning and declaring God's power, presence, and perspective – ultimately, God's purpose. Prophets hear a word, discern it, and declare it. Their emphasis is on the issue of power: the power of God, the presence of God, and the perspective of God for a specific person or a situation.

In the church, the prophet also provides leadership in areas of intercession, worship, and the use of spiritual gifts. The prophet not only prophesies to individuals and to the congregation, but he or she also prophesies God's direction to church leadership and apostolic leaders to help discern God's direction and will. The prophetic mandate is to help the Body of Christ grow in intimacy with God and holiness in life and to enjoy a greater experience of the presence and power of God.

Outside of the church, the natural prophetic gifting is often involved in the creative arts – in taking deeper thoughts and bringing them forth so that they can impact people in the source of their beings. Many people have said that artists like Bob Dylan were prophets because of their ability to reach deep places in their listeners' hearts with their lyrics.

Prophets awaken passion – that first-love desire for God, that desire to commune with His presence and to move in His power. Remember that there are different kinds of prophets. There are teaching prophets, pastoral prophets, and even apostolic prophets. As with all of the gifts, each can be expressed in different combinations and ways.

The Evangelistic Gift (Recruiter)

Declaring and Demonstrating the Gospel to Bring Conviction, Conversion, and Consecration to the Unreached

The evangelist is God's herald of the Good News of the Kingdom. This gift exists in a myriad of forms and expressions, from famous crusade evangelists who minister to thousands to the lowly street preacher who shares his or her faith with whoever will listen and respond. The evangelistic gift reveals itself in those who volunteer to serve the poor and those who share the love of Jesus with their next-door neighbors. This gift is empowered by a conviction of God's love and mercy for all and a deep longing that "none would perish but that all would come" to the knowledge of the truth.

Evangelism is first mentioned in Isaiah 52:7: .

"How beautiful upon the mountains
Are the feet of him who brings good news,
Who proclaims peace,
Who brings glad tidings of good things,
Who proclaims salvation, who says to Zion,
'Your God reigns!"

In this messianic passage, the prophet declares a blessing for those who would proclaim the Kingdom of God on the earth. Jesus personified that Good News as an evangelist who declared and demonstrated the Gospel of the Kingdom to bring conviction, conversion, and consecration to those who were yet unreached.

Evangelists declare the Gospel of the Kingdom; they understand it, they live it, and they can communicate it clearly. They can talk about all aspects of it. They can break it down into the language and culture of the people they are trying to reach. They also demonstrate the Gospel by caring for the poor, healing the sick, and casting out demons. Without a strong demonstration of God's power and love, we are just one more voice in the marketplace of ideas. But if there is a demonstration of love, commitment, service, self-sacrifice, deliverance, healing, and the binding up of broken hearts, then we will see people touched in a powerful way.

When the Gospel of the Kingdom comes, it should bring a sense of conviction in the heart of the person hearing it, which is then followed by conversion. Acts 2 shows us that combination: People saw the power of God demonstrated; they saw the phenomena, heard the different tongues, and then Peter stood up and preached. People cried out asking what to do and Peter answered, telling them to repent of their sins. They were brought into conviction; they saw that the lives they were living were below God's purposes for them, so they decided to yield their lives. Three thousand people were added to the church that day.

Evangelists share the Gospel of Jesus on a one-on-one basis, in small groups, on the streets, in businesses, through media, and at large conferences and even arena gatherings. Evangelists are passionate about reaching souls for Jesus, but they are also passionate about equipping the Church to reach the world. The evangelistic goal is that every single member would function evangelistically, that every member would know how to share his or her faith, how to lead people to Christ, and how to disciple people into a born-again experience in the Lord. This is the passion of the evangelist: to reach the lost and to equip the Church to do so as well.

The evangelist imparts both a passion to reach the lost and the tools for how to reach them. The best evangelists are those who can turn their knowledge or passion into practical tools.

Many evangelists have created programs to train people in how to reach the lost more effectively. One example of this that has been around for some time is the *Four Spiritual Laws* from Campus Crusade for Christ. Another example with a different approach is *The Way of the Master* by Ray Comfort. A more recent example that equips people in what John Wimber called "power evangelism" would be Kevin Dedmon's groundbreaking book *The Ultimate Treasure Hunt*. These are just a few examples of the many, many evangelistic tools out there.

There are many different evangelistic styles and models, but all of them empower believers with a passion for the lost and boldness to step out of their comfort zones in order to reach the unreached for Jesus.

Outside of the church, the unsaved evangelist aims to bring any good news about anything to everyone. These "evangelists" want everyone to do what they are doing, to like what they like, and to go where they go. They are often very persuasive in the way they communicate their passion. In business, they will likely lead people in sales, recruiting, or some kind of pronouncement of the bigger picture. In fact, many businesses have used the term "evangelist" as a job description for those in marketing and sales.

The Pastoral Gift (Connector)

Catalyzing and Cultivating a Christ-centered, Caring Community

God is the Shepherd and Caretaker of the flock; He has always intended that we should be in pastoral communities, and the Church of Jesus Christ was formed around a group of apostles who agreed to live in unity. The Church has always existed in community. We are a *body*; every member is interdependent upon one another. God has assigned shepherds to protect and uphold the body; these are the people we refer to as "pastors."

The pastoral gift catalyzes and cultivates a Christ-centered, caring community. Pastors are not necessarily responsible to pastor every person by themselves; rather, they release the dynamic of pastoral care into the community so that every member is caring for one another. That is where we get the "one another" passages of the Bible: love one another, care for one another, uphold one another, etc.

As I mentioned before, the word *pastor* is rarely used in the New Testament, but pastoral ministry was assigned to those who were called *elders*. In 1 Peter 5:1–3, Peter addresses the elders and describes their pastoral duties:

> The elders who are among you I exhort, I who am a fellow elder and a witness of the sufferings of Christ, and also a partaker of the glory that will be revealed: shepherd the flock of God which is among you, serving as overseers, not by compulsion but willingly, not for

dishonest gain but eagerly; nor as being lords over those entrusted to you, but being examples to the flock.

The Greek word meaning "elder" is the root of the English word *presbytery*. These are the more mature saints, and their mandate is to pastor and shepherd the flock for which God has given them oversight. The word for oversight is *episcopoi,* the root of our word *episcopal*. This word is also translated "bishop" or "supervisor." In this passage, a synonymous relationship exists among the words *elder, pastor,* and *bishop,* but later in the first century, the word *bishop* began to be used as a common substitute for the word *apostle.*

In the early church, elders were the leaders commissioned to provide pastoral care and shepherd the people of God, creating a sense of community and imparting the heart of God for one another in ministry.

In addition to the office of elder, the New Testament also presents one other position of leadership in the local church, and that is the office of deacon. Deacons are motivated by the same pastoral gift but express this gift in more practical ways. Whereas elders serve the people by providing pastoral care, deacons serve the community by facilitating projects and programs. Yet both are motivated by the pastoral impulse to see the believing community thrive and prosper in every way.

We see an example of that in Acts 6 when the apostles were overwhelmed with prayer and teaching the Word. When the crisis arose concerning the Greek widows not being served well, seven men who were filled with the Holy Spirit were chosen to oversee that issue. These men later became known as deacons. Some of them, such as Stephen and Philip, moved on to high levels of leadership.

Philip moved into an evangelistic role that reached Samaria in a powerful way. Stephen moved into more of a prophetic role and became the first martyr of the Church. Even though they ended up in very different roles, they both began as servants who cared for the projects and programs of the local church.

Probably the greatest manual of what a pastor is and what he is called to be is found in Psalm 23: "The LORD [is] my shepherd; I shall not want. He makes me to lie down in green pastures" (verses 1-2). That is what pastors do: They create an environment where people can rest, feed, and be watered well. They look out for the souls of the people they care for; they restore those souls and lead them in the paths of what is right for His name's sake. Even in the valley of the shadow of death (trials), the shepherd's rod and staff comfort the sheep and help them through those difficult periods. Pastors prepare a table of blessing for the sheep in the presence of the enemy, causing their cups to overflow. The result of effective pastoral ministry is that goodness and mercy surround the believer as he or she abides in the presence of the Lord.

This gift also functions outside the church through those who have not yet chosen to serve the Lord. It is a primary motivator of good parenting, professional counseling, social work, and medical care. Individuals with this gift are great team players and will often work in human resources or community services. This gift is also at work in those unique individuals who are natural connectors within their social group or workplace.

In summary, the pastoral gift is designed by God to cultivate caring community among His people, and it functions in several different ways. The first is by caring for people directly; the second is by equipping members of the community to care for each other, and the third is by serving the community in practical ways. Yet in each of these expressions, the community of believers is loved and cared for, protected and provided for. The pastoral gift infuses the community with the love of God and releases an atmosphere of acceptance and belonging.

The Teaching Gift (Trainer)

Communicating and Conveying Truth for Training and Transformation

Before we focus on this last gift, I would like to point out that some theologians say that the words *pastor* and *teacher* are hyphenated in Scripture and are therefore the same gift. I treat them as separate gifts for a very practical reason: I have met many great pastors who are not good teachers, and I have met many great teachers who are not very good pastors!

Teachers in the Body of Christ are called to instruct others and to be guardians of the truth. They understand Scripture, doctrine, and Church history. They understand the battles for truth that have been waged through history, and they protect truth by providing sound, biblical exegesis and expository teaching that help people grow in truth.

Teachers are also involved in specific mentoring of young believers that we often refer to as discipleship. They communicate and convey truth for training and transformation. The goal is not information; the goal is training and transformation. The teacher's function inside the church might be as a Bible study leader, disciple maker and teacher, even a Sunday morning preacher—all of these functions are ways of distributing and displaying the truth for training and transformation.

The primary goal of a teacher is to make disciples: whole-hearted followers of Jesus. This is accomplished by providing people with the basic, foundational truths that they need to become solid believers and followers of the Lord Jesus Christ. This passing of truth can happen on a one-on-one basis, in home groups, children's ministry, and Bible-study settings where teachers share the life-changing truths found in the Word of God.

Outside of the church, the teaching gift is usually seen in the role of a schoolteacher, instructor, professor, technical writer, etc. The teaching gift will manifest in many different ways, but teachers all love truth and love imparting it to the benefit of those who are listening.

Teachers are also equippers who impart their value for God's Word to others. They both teach others and train others to teach. They raise up people who love the Word and who are able to share the Word freely with others. This teaching gift is essential to the purposes of God. It may be the most important gift over the last twenty centuries because of the amount of error that threatened the Church, especially in the period before the canon of Scripture was fully decided upon.

Jesus was the ultimate teacher, and as we see Him teaching the Sermon on the Mount, instructing through parables, and giving the Upper Room discourse, He shares truth in a way that challenges the lies and misperceptions that reside in the hearts of His listeners. In a similar way, the apostle Paul and his teaching books provide amazing revelation and wisdom concerning the nature of our faith and the nature of God. The Book of Romans is a premier expression of Paul's teaching gift. He took the raw truths that Jesus had taught and formed them into a cohesive theology that impresses the most committed skeptics. Even secular logicians admit that there was a profound gift at work in Paul's life that allowed him to bring so much structure and framework to the truths that he presented.

How to Discover and Develop Your Ministry Gifts

These ministry gifts of Ephesians 4:11 provide the foundation for what we call your Destiny Orientation, or your *DO*. Your DO defines what you will "do" in every arena of life throughout your whole life. If you are an apostolic builder or a pastoral connector, it will flavor the way you interact at school, the way you parent your kids, the way you work at your job, and the way you minister at church.

As a reminder, there are two additional factors that will determine the impact of your Destiny Orientation: These are *scope* and *sphere*. Your scope of influence is the extent to which your DO will affect others. Some are called by God to be effective on a one-on-one basis and some in small groups; some will be most impactful on a congregational level and others on a regional or national scale. The question of sphere determines the branch of society that God has called you to influence.

How do you begin to discover and use these gifts?

First of all, pray for guidance in the discovery process. As you seek the Lord, He will continue to download the puzzle pieces of your destiny. He will provide revelation, prophetic impartation, and pastoral confirmation of your identity and destiny. He will make your calling and election sure.

Next, take the Destiny Finder online assessment at DestinyFinder.com. This tool will be very effective in helping you to discover your gift-mix and clarify your passions and dreams. Discuss your results with friends and mentors and see how God speaks to you through these various channels.

As you continue through the three phases of Destiny Finder and move from the Profiler to the Planner and Activator phases, you will find a growing ability to turn your personal vision into reality. We encourage you to continue through all of the Destiny Finder material and to locate coaches and mentors who will walk with you on this journey to fruitfulness and fulfillment.

May God give you understanding about His purpose for your life.

SEVEN
Your Motivational Orientation

As I mentioned before, my wife and I have seven children. One of the things that has surprised me most in having such a quiver-full is how utterly distinct and different they are from each other. Considering they were birthed from the same womb and raised in the same home by the same parents, you would expect more similarity. But God is the God of diversity. He specializes in making all things new.

Apart from the obvious differences between four boys and three girls, plus the various physical differences of height, build, eye and hair color, there is also the incredible diversity of talent and personality. There are different abilities and levels of creativity, intellect, articulation, and social skills. There are differing temperaments: One is easy going, and one is stubborn and strong-willed; one is decisive and opinionated . . . All of them are awesome.

In this chapter, we will focus on another category of gifting that is described in Romans 12. Most people refer to this category as the Motivational Gifts. As mentioned earlier, this list of gifts is different in context and focus from the other two lists of gifts. As a result, many would describe these gifts as personality, or temperament, gifts.

My ideas on this subject were drawn originally from Bill Gothard (Institutes in Basic Youth Conflicts) and have been shaped most recently by Gary Goodell, Director of Third Day Churches, who has contributed much to this chapter and the Destiny Finder survey.

In Destiny Finder, we refer to this group of gifts as the motivational orientations or the MO's, which is very similar to the common use of "MO," or *modus operandi*. Motivational gifts focus not so much on *what* you do but on the *way* in which you do it. Your MO describes the motivations that move you to action and the style of your interaction with others in life, ministry, and the workplace.

The Motivational Gifts

Just as each of us has one body with many members, and these members do not all have the same function, so in Christ we who are many form one body, and each member belongs to all the others. We have different gifts, according to the grace given us. If a man's gift is prophesying, let him use it in proportion to his[b] faith. [7] If it is serving, let him serve; if it is teaching, let him teach; [8] if it is encouraging, let him encourage; if it is contributing to the needs of others, let him give generously; if it is leadership, let him govern diligently; if it is showing mercy, let him do it cheerfully. (Romans 12:4-8 NIV)

This gift set describes the style through which we minister to others. The motivational gifts, like all of the various gifts of the Spirit, are given for the purpose of serving God. In order to serve God purely, our motivations must be transformed. In humility, we are to offer these gifts to God so that we may share them with others.

Paul writes in Romans 12:1:

> I beseech you therefore, brethren, by the mercies of God, that you present your bodies a living sacrifice, holy, acceptable to God, [which is] your reasonable service.

If we look at this passage through the eyes of destiny, we see that we have a role in presenting ourselves to God for His use. It is part of our partnership with Him. If we fail to step into that partnership, we restrict the best that God wants to bring forth in us.

As you present yourself to God, you might wonder, *Okay, a* living *sacrifice — how does that work?* A living sacrifice is alive but completely surrendered, completely yielded, and completely holy and acceptable unto God. We are called to give sacrificial service to Him. The word *service* in Romans 12:1 is one of two Greek words that are often translated "worship." The first word, *proskuneo,* is the word we most commonly use for "worship." It literally means to "turn toward and kiss." The second word used in this passage is *latreia,* and it was used to describe the acts of ritual worship that were carried out by the temple priests. This word indicates that everything we do in our lives can be transformed into an act of worship.

Romans 12:2 continues:

> And do not be conformed to this world, but be transformed by the renewing of your mind, that you may prove what [is] that good and acceptable and perfect will of God.

As living sacrifices, we are called to be living expressions of worship, but this depends on the renewal of our minds. As we discussed in an earlier chapter, we are told to take our thoughts captive to the obedience of Christ (2 Corinthians 10:5). As we do, we move from worldliness to godliness in our motivations and our actions, and we begin to do by nature the things that please God.

The motivational gifts we are about to look at are not separate from this process; as we renew our minds in relationship with our giftings, we will be able to prove with much more accuracy what is the good, acceptable, and perfect will of God.

Romans 12:3–5 continues:

> Do not think of yourself more highly than you ought, but rather think of yourself with sober judgment, in accordance with the measure of faith God has given you. Just as each of us has one body with many members, and these members do not all have the same function, so in Christ we who are many form one body, and each member belongs to all the others.

Let us look at the seven motivational gifts as found in Romans 12:6-8.

The Prophet (Perceiver)

"Prophet" is the one gift that occurs in all three of the biblical gift categories, so it deserves a bit more time to fully develop here. 1 Corinthians 12 mentions the gift of prophecy; Ephesians 4 establishes the office of a prophet, and Romans 12 includes the motivation of the prophet. This is the gift that anybody can access. As the Holy Spirit moves in a congregation, everyone can prophesy — this is confirmed by a clear, brief statement in 1 Corinthians 14:31: "For you can all prophesy." However, very few people will be deeply oriented toward the office of prophet. Those who have proven themselves consistent in the prophetic gift, and have demonstrated a true destiny calling toward that gift, will eventually be recognized by the Body of Christ by virtue of the consistency and impact of their giftings as prophets. We see many such people functioning today — either on a formal or informal basis.

The prophetic motivation is a way of viewing the world. Teachers will tend to be similar to prophets in that teachers will see things in terms of black and white, but their primary point of reference is Scripture itself or whatever text of knowledge they are citing. In other words, if I'm a teacher in my motivational orientation, I am going to be very precise in my understanding of God's Word, history, theology, doctrine, etc. From that precision, I will tend to be fairly unyielding when someone wants to tweak my understanding of the eternal purposes of God as revealed in Scripture.

A prophet is similar to a teacher, but the prophet's point of reference is different. It is no longer primarily the Word, although prophets love the Word. A prophet's point of reference is primarily the immediate, imminent interaction with the Holy Spirit. This is what we commonly call "revelation."

Prophets are oriented toward the presence, power, and purpose of the Spirit of God. They tend to develop a certain kind of clarity in the Spirit that appears almost black and white to those around them. Once they receive something from the Holy Spirit, it is very difficult for them to let it go or to compromise what they have seen because the revelation they have received becomes embedded in them as an issue of righteousness or unrighteousness, right or wrong. They see any compromise as an insult to the holiness, purity, or purpose of God.

Prophetic people tend to stand on the mountain, call people up to that higher place, and never settle for second best.

The Minister (Server)

Minister is the word from which we get *deacon*. The original use is not like our contemporary idea of a pastor-minister but more like that of a servant. As a server, you serve according to the heart that God has given you.

Romans 12:10 gives an example of this service: "Love each other with genuine affection, and take delight in honoring each other." The server is always looking for practical ways to show love through acts of service. Servers are motivated by needs or problems they can help fix. As a simple example, people with a Server MO may see the pastor standing at the copy machine on Sunday morning and ask, "Hey, can I make your copies for you?"

The people operating from this gift will see a task and volunteer to take care of it. They take their time, energy, and talent and apply them as the answer to whatever the problem, issue, or need is.

Because servers are often motivated by unmet needs and uncompleted tasks, they can be misperceived as workaholics, as performance-oriented, or as trying to brown-nose their way into winning the favor of others. But the heart of the gift is to love through service. Jesus says that the greatest among us would be the servant of all, and this gifting reflects that charge. The ministering servant heart does not respond to the needs of others out of duty or obligation but as an expression of love.

The Teacher or Instructor

Teachers see the world primarily in terms of fact and falsehood, accuracy and error. They are motivated to bring knowledge and overcome ignorance. People with a Teacher MO are usually disciplined and focused. They typically keep a clean calendar and a balanced checkbook. They are obsessed with truth and are intolerant of sloppy theology and a casual approach to biblical interpretation.

When they see someone who doesn't know something, they desire to bring knowledge into that situation. Because of that, they are often perceived as know-it-alls, but they are driven by accuracy and by helping people out of darkness. Teachers are riled by error and desire to bring truth and therefore *quality* into every situation that seems important to them. We need teachers in our lives because they clarify the things that are unclear.

The Exhorter or Encourager

Exhorters stir people up and spur them on; they are motivated to motivate. They are motivated when they see unrealized potential because they want to see people achieving their best. Exhorters will challenge you to go to the next level.

Romans 12:12 illustrates the exhorter's attitude of rejoicing in confident hope. No case is a hopeless case to the exhorter. Though they are often misperceived as simplistic or as throwing out simple answers to complex problems, exhorters are constantly looking at people through the lens of hope; they see other people's destinies and propel them on to achieve them.

The Giver

Givers are motivated by a lack of resources and the physical needs of those around them. They respond with care, concern, and the necessary resources to meet those needs. It is their passion to make sure everyone is well supplied. Similar to ministers, givers are motivated by need, but they tend to see the real need as material and therefore specifically step in to provide material resources. If something is needed, they are there to supply it.

Givers are the ones who pull over to the side of the road, roll down the driver's window, and hand cash to the guy standing there with a cardboard sign. They often support foreign missionaries, local ministries, and are sure to write as many checks as they can to provide for the needs that are presented in their church.

Because they are so willing to give away what they have, givers can be misperceived as gullible "doormats" or as people who are easily taken advantage of. They see a need and give whatever they can to supply that need; the giver does not want anyone to go without, especially not when it is within his or her power to provide.

The Leader

The effective leader is both visionary and diligent. Leaders are motivated by unachieved corporate outcome. They know that if we work together, we can be ten times greater than if we work alone, so they are constantly striving to connect people to each other and to the goals of the organization. Leaders are often good delegators; they know how to bring people together, get them focused, and assign tasks. They can see how the different gifts fit into the whole. They can often be misperceived as manipulative or exploitive because of their ability to see how people work best and their tendency to tell people what to do. They are born to take charge!

The Comforter

The comforter sees pain and suffering and seeks to remove them. They are motivated by mercy and often have difficulty seeing people as sinners but tend to see people as victims. They are filled with empathy and forgive others easily. This can make them vulnerable to manipulation by those who are deceptive or who cover their faulty characters with excuses and self-justifications. Because of this, they can sometimes be misperceived as non-confrontational or codependent. They extend mercy with a cheerful heart.

Comforters make great listeners and counselors. They carry the heart of Jesus expressed in the statement, "The Spirit of the LORD [is] upon Me, because He has . . . sent Me to heal the broken-hearted" (Luke 4:18). They also reflect the opening lines of 2 Corinthians:

> Blessed [be] the God . . . of all comfort, who comforts us in all our tribulation that we may be able to comfort those who are in trouble with the same comfort wherewith we have been comforted of God.

Comforters do not let their own needs get in the way of making someone else feel better.

How to Discover Your Motivational Gifts

Your Motivational Orientation is woven into the fabric of your personality and shaped by the formative forces of life, and this is why it may be hard to recognize or identify. Sometimes it is hard to see the forest for the trees. Yet with the help of some discovery tools and the input of a few good friends, your motivational gifts will become clear. As you discover your MO and the MO's of those around you, we encourage you to remember not to use this understanding to put yourself or others in a box. Rather, celebrate the unique design that God has given to each of us.

So how do we discover and develop our motivational gifts? The first part of the discovery process is prayer. Ask God to show you and confirm for you how He has wired you, and then thank Him for what He, in His perfect wisdom, has given you.

Second, after you take the Destiny Finder online assessment, share the results with friends and mentors. Ask them if your results line up with how they see you, remembering that gift discovery is a process that unfolds over time.

Finally, I cannot emphasize enough how important community is. Community keeps us real. It keeps us from getting bogged down in our weaknesses, and it offers a support network to help us as we reach our potential. You will benefit the most when you invite people to participate in your process and when you participate in theirs.

In Conclusion

As we wrap up this chapter, I would like to concentrate a bit more on the relationship between the three dimensions of spiritual gifts. At the end of 1 Corinthians 12, Paul begins to provide a framework for understanding the relationship between various gifts:

> And God has appointed in the church, first apostles, second prophets, third teachers, and after that miracles, then gifts of healings, helps, administrations and varieties of tongues (1 Corinthians 12:28).

The first thing to notice in this list is that Paul declares a hierarchy in the relationship of apostles, prophets, and teachers. He also puts the ministry gifts ahead of the other two sets of gifts.

In addition, Paul integrates the three different groups of gifts in this list. He adds two words that do not occur in the other lists. In the New King James Version (which we use here), they are translated "helps" and "administrations." The word *helps* is almost identical to the (Romans 12) word *ministry* or *service*, and the word *administrations* is just as similar to the word *lead* found in Romans 12. It is interesting that Paul is not as concerned about the actual words or terminology as he is about the functional meaning. On the basis of this, I do consider these two new words to be a reiteration of the words found in the motivational gifts.

EIGHT
Your Spiritual Orientation

About twenty years ago, I had the unique opportunity to spend time with a man who told me about his experience in an unusual outpouring of the Holy Spirit. In 1948, God began to move in a powerful way among certain churches along the Canadian border. These churches believed in the work of the Spirit, but they had no grid for the way in which the Lord began to move among them. During this season, the gifts of the Holy Spirit were activated in every single member in very precise and specific ways, and every believer began to minister in supernatural power. In many instances, if you had a problem, you could go to an individual who was anointed to break the power of that particular problem, and you would be delivered from it.

For example, let us say you had an addiction to nicotine; the person gifted in breaking that specific addiction would pray for you, and you would be freed from that addiction. Or if you suffered from a spiritual or emotional wounding, somebody else would have a gift-mix combo that could break the power of whatever torment, fear, sadness, or depression you were dealing with. If you had a cancer or tumor in your body, someone would be uniquely anointed to touch that area and see healing released.

Then in 1950, these churches began to experience a diminishment of God's presence and power. As this season came to an end, God told the leadership that He had released this amazing season of miracles among them to give them a foretaste of what would happen in the last days. The Lord assured them that a time is coming when all believers will know their gifts and callings and be able to function fully in the manifestation of the Holy Spirit's power for the blessing of many. It is our conviction that this word is being fulfilled before our eyes.

The Spiritual Gifts

If you have been born again, you have the Holy Spirit living within you. If the Holy Spirit is within you, then you have access to every gift and blessing that the Holy Spirit has to give. These gifts are given to empower you to minister to others, both in the Church and beyond. They are powerful expressions of a powerful God. Although these gifts have been a point of controversy and even contention, they are important and worth taking time to study and appreciate. We need all that God has for us in order to accomplish His purposes in the earth.

Your gifts are intended to bless and bring out the best in others. Your gifts provide nourishment and nutrition, vision and blessing, support and healing to others. In 1 Corinthians 12:4-11, Paul gives us the context for these ministry gifts:

There are diversities of gifts, but the same Spirit. There are differences of ministries, but the same Lord. And there are diversities of activities, but it is the same God who works all in all. But the manifestation of the Spirit is given to each one for the profit [of all]: for to one is given the **word of wisdom** through the Spirit, to another the **word of knowledge** through the same Spirit, to another **faith** by the same Spirit, to another **gifts of healings** by the same Spirit, to another the **working of miracles**, to another **prophecy**, to another **discerning of spirits**, to another [different] **kinds of tongues**, to another the **interpretation of tongues**. But one and the same Spirit works all these things, distributing to each one individually as He wills. (NIV)

Since we all have the same Holy Spirit, we can *all* use *all* of these gifts. We can all pray for somebody and deliver a gift of healing. We can all speak in tongues. We can all receive words of knowledge or wisdom and discern spirits, etc. God distributes His gifts to us so we can touch others in His name. Although each of us can operate in every gift, each one of us will tend to function in one or two of these gifts more exclusively according to our unique design. This third dimension of spiritual gifting provides anointing and power to fulfill the promise of Jesus that "greater things shall you do because I go to the Father."

So let us look at each of these spiritual gifts in detail:

Word of Wisdom (*Logos Sophia*)

The word *wisdom* means "applied knowledge." The word of wisdom usually appears as "divine problem solving." Solomon provides a good Old Testament example of someone who often operated in the word of wisdom. He once was confronted with a dispute between two women. One woman's baby had died in the night, and she had secretly changed babies with the other woman. Both women appeared before Solomon the next day to have him judge the situation.

Solomon offered a harsh but revealing solution: "Let's cut the baby in half and give each woman one piece."

The mother who had stolen the baby agreed because she had already lost her baby.

But the true mother said, "No! Don't do that! Give the baby to her."

Solomon was immediately able to discern the true mother by her response.

In the New Testament, we see Peter sitting at the tanner's house in Joppa. He was about to be confronted with a problem, and the Lord gave him wisdom about it beforehand. Peter saw a sheet being let down from Heaven with all kinds of unclean animals in it. The Lord told him to kill and eat.

Immediately after the vision, a messenger appeared at his door. This messenger was sent by a Roman leader named Cornelius, who requested that Peter come and tell him about the Truth. Of course, a Jew was not allowed to enter the house of a centurion because Gentiles were considered unclean people, but God had just given him a word of wisdom about how to deal with this problem. The meaning of the word was obvious to Peter: Just as he was told to consider unclean animals the same as clean animals, he was to accept the Gentiles as he would the Jewish people. They were to be given the same opportunity to receive the Gospel.

When you receive a word of wisdom, you receive a supernatural impartation from God's Spirit that gives you the ability to resolve issues and problems.

Word of Knowledge (*Logos Gnosis*)

Knowledge is information. A word of knowledge is information that you could not have known naturally; therefore, it is supernatural information.

When Jesus looked up into the sycamore tree and saw Zacchaeus, there is no indication that He had previously met the man. Yet Jesus called him by name and said, "I am going to have lunch at your house today." How did Jesus know his name?

Remember the story of Ananias and Sapphira? They sold their property for the contemporary equivalent of a million dollars and gave half of it to the church, which was a generous gift. However, they lied to the church, telling them that they were giving 100 percent of the sale's proceeds. Peter had a clear word of knowledge that they were lying, and they ended up dead. The word of knowledge is a powerful tool.

Once, Diane and I were praying for a Chinese girl who was tormented by demons. After a couple of difficult hours of ministry, we turned to the Lord for greater understanding. Suddenly, a string of Chinese words came to my wife's mind. She just "read" them off phonetically as she looked at them in her mind with her eyes closed. These words were the girl's mother's maiden name! This word of knowledge was the key to setting this young woman free. She went on to tell Diane that her mother had gotten pregnant out of wedlock and wanted to marry the baby's father. She thought she was having a miscarriage and knew the man would not marry her if she lost the baby, so she went to the temple priest and had the baby dedicated. This opened a level of demonic access in the girl's life. We prayed with this knowledge in mind, and the girl was set free.

Faith (*Pistis*)

The gift of faith ("I believe God can do this") is distinguished from saving faith ("I believe that Jesus died for my sins, so I gave my life to Him"). The gift of faith is the kind that can move mountains. Peter, in the midst of a stormy night on the Sea of Galilee, operated in this gift when he stepped out of the boat and walked on water.

My wife and I once encountered a woman who had one foot that was two inches longer than the other. Diane was immediately confident that a healing was about to happen, and she called everyone over to witness what God was about to do. This woman was instantly healed and had to take off her shoes to go home because the heels had been adjusted to compensate for her uneven legs. Diane received a gift of faith, and the result was a miracle.

This does not necessarily mean that every person who proclaims, "I am going to be healed!" will instantly be healed, but there is a connection between seeing miracles happen and the gift of faith—actively believing God can do something.

Gift of Healings (*Charisma Iama*)

The gift of healing is the dispensation of God's healing power for physical, mental, and spiritual restoration. A great example of this gift is found with Peter and John at the gate Beautiful when they said to the lame man, "Silver and gold I do not have, but what I do have I give you: In the name of Jesus Christ of Nazareth, rise up and walk" (Acts 3:6). The man went away walking and leaping and rejoicing because of his healing.

God loves everyone and desires to heal the whole person: body, emotions, and mind. Jesus ministered healing to hundreds of people in Scripture, and He continues to do so today. All around the world, there are amazing testimonies of people being healed of everything from back problems to terminal cancer. God continues to demonstrate His power through the gift of healings operating through His people.

Working of Miracles (Energema Dunamis)

The working of miracles is the demonstration of power over nature and natural things: water turning into wine, loaves and fishes multiplying, raising the dead. A miracle is a supernatural intervention of God.

Years ago, I was driving my family home from Lake Tahoe, and we were the first people at the site of an accident on Carquinez Bridge. Right in front of us, a drunken woman had plowed into the center divider and had been thrown from her car. We stopped our van in the middle of the freeway to block traffic and went to check on her.

The woman was dead; she wasn't breathing and she had no pulse. She reeked of alcohol. We thought, *This is not God's will for this woman to die in this way,* so we began to pray. There was no doctor to tell us what to do, so we called on the Great Physician to intervene. We prayed and commanded her to come back to life, and all of a sudden, she started breathing. It was phenomenal. God worked through us to miraculously bring a woman back to life.

Prophecy (*Propheteia*)

The gift of prophecy is the ability to speak the anointed words of God. According to 1 Corinthians 14, the primary use of the gift of prophecy is for edification, exhortation, and comfort. Edify means to "build up"; exhort means to "stir up," and comfort means to "bind up." This gift is not to be confused with the *calling*, or office, of a prophet, which is developed and proven over many years of prophetic ministry. This basic gift of prophecy is available to everyone, no matter the person's age or maturity. Even a new believer can function in the general gift of prophecy as long as it edifies, exhorts, and comforts.

On the other hand, the calling of a prophet includes additional elements, such as correction and direction. An example of this can be found in Acts 13. Some prophets and teachers had gathered, and the Spirit spoke, instructing them to send Paul and Barnabas out to do the work God had called them to. So they fasted, prayed, and sent Paul and Barnabas out as He had said.

Another example of the prophetic call occurred with a man named Agabus, who I mentioned earlier. He went to a town and declared under the anointing of the Spirit, "There is going to be a great famine in the land." People responded to the word and prepared for the famine, even though they had no evidence that the prophecy was going to be fulfilled. They were saved as a result of Agabus' prophetic warning.

Those who are called to serve as recognized prophets have all begun their ministry journeys by functioning in the spiritual gift of prophecy. Although most of those who function in this gift will not become recognized prophetic leaders, this gift is a training ground for aspiring prophetic leaders to improve their ability to hear the voice of God and serve the Church on God's behalf. There are dozens of examples in the New Testament of individuals who operated in the gift of prophecy.

It is time for the Body of Christ to realize that our God is a living God and He longs to communicate directly to His people through these spiritual gifts. These gifts do not undermine our love for the Bible. On the contrary, the Bible commands us not to despise prophecy. We need to welcome these gifts, provide oversight and correction when needed, and mentor these individuals into their destinies.

Discerning of Spirits (Diakrisis Pneuma)

The Greek words *diakrisis pneuma* literally mean "discerning spirits." This is the ability to discern whether something someone says or does has its origin in a demonic, human, or divine source. There are many examples in Scripture where Jesus and the apostles discerned whether something was demonic or not. After Peter declared who Jesus was, Jesus replied, "Flesh and blood has not revealed this to you, but My Father who is in heaven" (Matthew 16:17). In other words, Jesus discerned the source of Peter's understanding.

This likely was encouraging for Peter, but unfortunately, a few verses later, Jesus told Peter that He

(Jesus) was going to be killed in Jerusalem. Peter rebuked Him, and Jesus replied, "Get behind Me, Satan! You are an offense to Me, for you are not mindful of the things of God, but the things of men" (Matthew 16:23). It is interesting that in the span of a single chapter, Jesus ascribed the source of Peter's revelation to the Father and the source of his next statement to Satan.

Another example of the discerning of spirits can be found in Acts 13 where Peter rebuked Elymas the sorcerer. In the story of Ananias and Sapphira (Acts 5), Peter asked them how they had allowed the devil to bewitch them. These are just a few of the numerous examples of discernment found throughout Scripture. It was important then, and it is certainly important now.

Discerning of spirits can be a tricky gift to operate in if you are not abiding in and getting your discernment from the Father. I have been in situations in which people appeared to be manifesting demons, but they actually were expressing deep roots of pain in their lives that caused them to react strongly and be out of control. In another situation, while ministering to a person who was truly demonized, I was told by the person during a break, "Everything's all right. The demons are gone." But in my spirit, I sensed that was not true, and I realized that the demon was speaking through the person, trying to get us to stop praying.

I once knew a young man who was coming out of witchcraft. He had been attending our church for a while when we were able to pray for him, and he seemed to have been set free. Then a few months later, I discerned that he was still involved in Satan worship. That understanding just came to my spirit. I challenged him on it, and he confessed that yes, he had been returning to the Satanist meetings. In fact, there was a plot against our church, and the group had lured him back to be an agent of cursing toward our church. Thankfully, God always leads us into truth and triumph in Christ Jesus.

Kinds of Tongues (*Genos Glossa*)

The gift of speaking in other tongues is a tool for communicating the Gospel in other languages as well as a method of prophecy, prayer, and praise. In the Scriptures, we have two dimensions of the gift of tongues: One is private and personal in nature, while the other is for public use. In this book, I am primarily talking about the public use of this gift, although the private gift of tongues is, at some level, included in this understanding.

In his letters, Paul tells us a few things about tongues that are helpful to keep in mind. For instance, everyone can operate in this gift; tongues are a sign of God's presence, and they should not be used in a public setting without an interpretation (1 Corinthians 14:18-28). Also, Paul indicates that when people speak in tongues, they are not necessarily speaking existing human languages. In 1 Corinthians 13, he uses the phrase, "If I speak with tongues of men and tongues of *angels* . . ."

In Acts 2:4, this gift was expressed in human language when the different nations who had gathered for Pentecost heard the disciples speaking in their tongues. We don't know whether they were speaking in the tongues of those nations or whether the Holy Spirit—through interpretations—was able to help the individuals hear what was being spoken in their own languages. Whether it was one or the other, it was still an amazing miracle.

We find that same miracle throughout history. There are many examples of individuals who have spoken in a tongue they did not know. The group of Blackfeet Indians I lived with as a new believer experienced a situation in which a white man came to preach and began to speak to them in perfect Blackfeet. He had no previous knowledge of that language, and the encounter caused many to believe.

As I said, the gift of tongues can be an actual tongue of man or that of angels. In 1 Corinthians 14:14 and Jude 1:20, we see that when we speak in tongues, we actually build up our spiritual strength because we speak to God in mysteries. Some people believe that this gift, when given in public, should be interpreted as a prayer—not as prophecy—because 1 Corinthians 14 says, "We speak to God." Others disagree with that, but either way, the gift of tongues was given as a sign of the Holy Spirit among us. In Acts 10, Cornelius and his household received the gift of tongues before they formally accepted Jesus or were baptized. The Spirit of God came upon the household, and they were able to speak in other tongues.

Some Christians would say that tongues are the primary sign of the Holy Spirit's presence in an individual. Whether or not that is true, we certainly know that tongues have value. The primary value of private tongues is to edify the individual who is speaking in them; they are almost like a bypass of our mental faculties that gets us more directly in touch with the Lord. We could also reference Romans 8, which says that we don't know how to pray as we should, but the Holy Spirit helps us by giving us utterances that cannot be vocalized. These utterances, or "groanings," include but are not limited to tongues.

Jesus says, "He who believes in Me, as the Scripture has said, out of his heart will flow rivers of living water" (John 7:38). Then the passage goes on to say, "He spoke concerning the Holy Spirit." Tongues reach the deep cores of our beings and can manifest in languages we don't naturally know so that we can release what the Lord is doing deep within us.

The apostle Paul gives a tremendous amount of attention to talking about the value of tongues in a public meeting without interpretation. In fact, he says that tongues shouldn't be used publicly in a gathering without interpretation because they aren't intelligible and thus do not edify. He says he would rather that everyone prophesy or speak a word in a known language than a thousand words in tongues because tongues have limited value unless they are interpreted. With that said, the need for interpretation of tongues becomes evident.

Interpretation of Tongues (Hermeneia Glossa)

This is the supernatural ability to interpret an unknown language. Sometimes this gift is used to interpret the language of another people group — for example, a man who comes into an unfamiliar culture where he does not understand the language, but God enables him to understand it through the gift of interpretation. Mostly, though, this gift pertains to someone speaking in tongues in a congregational meeting where another person has the interpretation.

This is not a translation but rather an understanding

of what the tongues is intended to say. So whether it is an earthly language being used (a tongue of man) or a tongue of angels, we don't apply a kind of Rosetta Stone process. Instead, we have the Holy Spirit, who actually gives us an understanding of what was said, not necessarily a word-for-word translation.

In most cases where I have heard the gift of tongues used publicly, the interpretations were interpreted as prophecy. These were "Thus sayeth the Lord" types of statements to the congregation on God's behalf. However, I have also heard interpretation of tongues in the form of a prayer: speaking to God on behalf of the congregation or an individual in the congregation. This is why 1 Corinthians 14:12 tells us that we need to let "him who speaks in a tongue pray that he may interpret." I find this interesting because it seems to indicate also that the interpreter can be the individual who actually speaks in a tongue. Then the question becomes: Why would the person speak in tongues if he or she can just pray or prophesy in the known language?

In verses 14–15, we find the answer:

> For if I pray in a tongue, my spirit prays, but my understanding is unfruitful. What is [the conclusion] then? I will pray with the spirit, and I will also pray with the understanding. I will sing with the spirit, and I will also sing with the understanding.

In these cases Paul is saying, "Go for it. Go for tongues, but don't disrupt the meeting, and don't prophesy or pray out loud in tongues in a public meeting unless there's an interpretation."

Intelligibility is the interpretive key to Paul's counsel in this chapter. In a public meeting around the uninitiated,

Paul wants there to be a maximized intelligibility. It is important for us to understand how to interpret tongues so that everyone is built up. The interpretation of tongues is a valuable gift that God has given us, but as it is with speaking in tongues, there are considerations about how it should be governed.

This might be a good place to mention other "unintelligible" things such as physical "manifestations." I have been in many settings in which the presence of God was so strong that it caused physical responses. This is what I playfully refer to as "physiological tongues." These phenomena can take the form of falling, shaking, weeping, or laughter.

An amazing example of this kind of physical encounter with God is the story of Heidi Baker, a missionary who served for many years with very little fruit. However, around fifteen years ago, she experienced a dramatic encounter with God in which she was physically impacted and even incapacitated. Since that time, she and her husband, Rolland, have pioneered a movement in Africa that has grown to over 10,000 churches, innumerable salvations, and thousands of amazing healings.

Although very few have had this kind of impact after an encounter with God, most experience some tangible spiritual benefits. In fact, these physical responses to God's presence have been a part of almost every revival throughout history; they may be hard to understand, but they often have great spiritual value. Jonathan Edwards, one of the leaders of the First Great Awakening, wrote extensively on these things and counseled his readers not to judge the "spiritual affections" by their appearance but by the fruit they bore in the life of the believer.

Do such things bring us closer to Jesus, or do they take us further away? That is the biblical litmus test concerning manifestations that we don't immediately understand. Jesus says, "You shall know them by their fruits." I believe it is helpful to apply the scriptural commands of Paul concerning the interpretation of tongues to our understanding of other physical manifestations as well.

How to Walk in the Gifts of the Spirit

As we conclude our look at the gifts of the Spirit, it is clear that God has provided a toolbox full of "power tools" to help us fulfill the ministry of Jesus on the earth. In fact, when Jesus was about to ascend, He told His disciples to "wait in Jerusalem until power comes upon you from on high. Then you shall be My witnesses..." This command and promise were fulfilled on the Day of Pentecost, as the Holy Spirit was poured out on the early Church.

How do we use all of these gifts? First, we receive the gifts of the Holy Spirit when we receive the Holy Spirit Himself. When we are born again, we have the Holy Spirit living in us:

> But you are not in the flesh but in the Spirit, if indeed the Spirit of God dwells in you. Now if anyone does not have the Spirit of Christ, he is not His (Romans 8:9).

If we have the Spirit of God, then He is *in* us. We also understand from Scripture that there are different levels of intensity in the Holy Spirit's work. I believe that God desires His people to have many encounters with the Holy Spirit throughout their lives. Ephesians 5:18 instructs, "Do not be drunk with wine, in which is dissipation; but be filled with the Spirit." That idea of being filled is a Greek verb tense that means "to be continually re-filled."

So the first step toward walking in the gifts of the Spirit is to ask the Lord for a greater infilling. If you have received the Spirit, then ask Him to give you more and more. We need to seek the Giver but *also* the gifts. There is no conflict between the two because, ultimately, the gifts empower us to seek the Giver and the Giver, by definition, always comes with gifts.

In Jeremiah 19:13, we read, "You will seek Me and find [Me], when you search for Me with all your heart." In the New Testament, Jesus echoes this:

> "So I say to you, ask, and it will be given to you; seek, and you will find; knock, and it will be opened to you. For everyone who asks receives, and he who seeks finds, and to him who knocks it will be opened" (Luke 11:9–10).

The conclusion of this passage is in verse 13: "How much more will [your] heavenly Father give the Holy Spirit to those who ask Him!"

As you pray, study, worship, and seek the Lord, invite Him to come into your heart in deeper and deeper ways. He promises that He will give you the Holy Spirit if you ask.

A second step is learning to discern the voice of God. I cannot stress this point enough. The most common misconception concerning spiritual gifts is that they will come to us so forcefully or God will speak so loudly that it will overwhelm us. Actually, the opposite is true. Because we are unaccustomed to hearing the voice of God and we are unfamiliar with the guidance of the Spirit, we often miss what God wants to do. The gifts of God become clearer and louder the more we exercise them.

Hebrews 5:14 tells us, "But solid food belongs to those who are of full age, [that is], those who by reason of *use* have their senses exercised to discern both good and evil." We can train our inner ear to hear the Lord accurately. Like the mechanic who can hear a car and understand whether it is idle, healthy, or missing a cylinder—we can tune ourselves to hear the Holy Spirit.

Third, we need to start actually ministering in the spiritual gifts; we cannot just receive and then walk away. Start praying for everyone you can. Ask the Lord for words of knowledge and wisdom—give words, step out, and take risks. Be willing to be wrong in order to learn to discern between good and evil in terms of what the Lord is saying and what He is not saying.

Take every opportunity to minister to others— Sundays at church, home groups, the market, and the marketplace. Ask anyone who is ill if he or she would like prayer right then and there. Try to discern what spirit someone is operating in and ask the Lord to speak to you and confirm what is going on. The more you practice, the better you get.

If you show up at the Big Leagues without ever having practiced baseball, you are never going to play at the level you would like. But if you build yourself up through Little League, high school baseball, college baseball, and hours and hours of practice, you might just be able to stand on a pitcher's mound someday and throw that perfect pitch.

Everything in life that is worth doing requires practice, whether you are playing an instrument, singing a song, teaching a class, or operating in the gifts of the Spirit. Take risks; don't be afraid of making mistakes, and keep trying, trying, trying. The people who heal the sick are the ones who have tried a thousand times and maybe half as many times haven't seen results, but the more they applied themselves, the more they found themselves moving forward.

In Conclusion

We began this chapter by talking about how God intends His spiritual gifts to function. All followers of Jesus have the capacity to operate in every gift of the Spirit, yet because we are all wired differently, we will tend to function in one or two of these gifts more than the others. So no single believer can fully reflect and represent Jesus. We need one another.

Throughout this book, we have stressed that each one of us is part of the *Body* of Christ. Just as the human body cannot be healthy and whole if it is cut in pieces, so we, as individual members of Christ, cannot live as He intended without being connected to the other members. In addition, to the extent that we fail to understand our need for one another, we will always be limited in our impact on the world around us.

In the next chapter, we are going to look at passions and dreams and how God uses them to guide us forward in destiny.

NINE

Passion and Dream

As I mentioned before, I was raised in the counter-culture of the 1960's, and as a believer, I have always been intrigued by God's heart toward emerging culture. I grew up as part of that culture, and in my early twenties as an evangelistic minister in San Francisco, I spent most of my time ministering among that culture. During that time, I was able to experience God's heart toward these individuals, and my passion was seized.

However, as the years passed and I became the pastor of a growing church, I found myself having to withdraw a bit from that passion. It became increasingly necessary for me to focus on running the church, caring for members, and training and mobilizing leaders. As a result, my passion and dream for reaching emerging culture began to become diffused, and that piece of my heart began to die.

Then in the early 1990's, a few people in our church decided to begin a ministry on Haight Street, which was the epicenter of the hippie movement that began about thirty years prior. God began to move powerfully through our team, and they began to see a harvest of these young "neo-hippies" coming to the Lord. Our team eventually got a house on Ashbury and began to serve the community with food, clothing, prayer, and the Gospel of the Kingdom.

My heart for emerging culture began to be re-ignited as we saw dozens of young people give their lives to Jesus. We started a discipleship program; sent teams on tour with different "jam bands"; and hosted large, successful events that gained us much notoriety. *The 700 Club* eventually interviewed us, and as a result, we were given a parcel of beautiful land in the redwoods by a woman who was awakened by the Lord in the middle of the night and saw our interview. We also began to hear about counter-cultural travelers who were gathering in key places around the world, and so we began to lead teams to Thailand, India, Israel, and Europe to minister among the international traveler scene.

The more I renewed my passion for emerging culture, the more alive I began to feel. In 2000 with twenty students, we launched a fledgling school called AIM: the Advanced Institute of Ministry. The focus of this school was to train ministry pioneers within the various branches of emerging culture. Each of the different subcultures was represented: hip-hop and spoken word, neo-hippie, punk rock, rave scene, and the student world. We started a handful of ministries to these various groups and saw some amazing fruit. We continued the school for several years and began to fully understand what it takes to reach and disciple the coming harvest. This piece of my history illustrates the ways in which our Kingdom dreams and passions contribute to our personal destinies.

My Passion Statement

My primary passion in life is to prepare God's people for the coming revival and the billion-soul harvest. The reason I care so much about emerging culture is the fact that the vast majority of those who come to Christ do so before turning twenty-five. The coming harvest will be predominantly young. Those who will reach and disciple this harvest must be prepared for discipleship challenges that the Church has never encountered before. That is why I am so passionate about ministering to the young.

This passion has continued to drive my destiny discovery and has led me to a point where I now serve an amazing global youth ministry called Jesus Culture as the director of development. Every step along the way, I have seen God's hand guiding me forward. I am partnered with a gifted younger leader named Banning Liebscher, the director of Jesus Culture, who is being used by God to transform a generation through catalytic events and some of the most amazing worship music on the planet. And I get to be a part of all of this.

In this chapter, we will discover that our passions and dreams are not insignificant steps on the journey to fulfilling our destinies. In fact, they are often the clearest indicator of what God has called us to do. As we talked about in the last few chapters, God gives each of us a specific gift-mix, but He also gives us the *desire* to step into the callings He has for us. In order for us to endure the challenges and changes necessary to discover and fulfill our callings, destiny has to be something we want— something that is pressing and urgent in our hearts—and not merely a task we feel compelled to do. For this reason,

God hardwires destiny into our hearts in the form of dreams and desires that propel us in the right direction.

Sadly, this has proven to be a difficult concept for some Christians to grasp. For whatever reason, many believers assume that our Father is a cruel taskmaster. They think that if they really gave themselves fully to God's purposes, He would assign us to something entirely unpleasant; something contrary to our natural likes and dislikes. But that is a mistaken concept. This is not to say that *everything* we desire is God's desire for us. Our human ambitions and aspirations are subject to many other influences besides the Holy Spirit. Still, spiritual passions remain one of the principle keys to unlocking our destinies.

God Uses Our Dreams

As we begin to drill deeper into the concept of Kingdom dreams and desires, one of the first things I need to address is a common misunderstanding in the Body of Christ. Because of the doctrine of total depravity, many believers tend to look at the human heart in an entirely negative light. We often apply this thought process to ourselves as Christians, and we certainly apply it to the lost. We tend to think, *'There is no possibility of any good thing in that person.'*

However, Scripture actually gives us a slightly different picture. I am *not* suggesting that sin does not exist or that it hasn't poisoned and alienated the human heart, but I am suggesting that there are other aspects that need to be considered.

For instance, in the parable of the sower and the seed, Jesus goes through the different types of soils that resist the Holy Spirit and God's Kingdom within a person's life. But then He gets to the final soil, the soil that receives the seed and ultimately produces a harvest—"some hundredfold, some sixty, some thirty." He says, "That seed is the good and honest heart" (Luke 8:15).

We have to ask ourselves, *How did a person acquire a good and honest heart apart from Christ to receive the seed that grows up into Christ?* In other words, there must be some dimension in which God perceives us, even in our unconverted state, as having some sincerity and honest intent.

Paul underscores this in Romans 1–2 when he talks about the heathen who do by nature the things the law requires, even though they don't know the law. Based on that verse, there can be some active work of conscience in the heart of humanity that helps us respond positively to God, despite our continued struggles with sin and brokenness in our lives.

When I was a young believer, I often heard, "God doesn't hear the prayers of the wicked!" But look at the story of Cornelius, who, as you remember, was a Roman centurion. Here was a man who prayed and shared his wealth with the people of Israel. Scripture calls him a "devout man," even though he did not have a personal relationship with Jesus.

The Lord sent an angel to tell him, "God has heard your prayers and seen your alms that you have given toward His people, and He has arranged salvation for you."

This all being said, it is clear that God can use our passions and dreams to help guide us in life. That doesn't mean those passions and dreams are 100 percent aligned with the destiny God has for each of us, especially when we are young believers. But it does mean that in one way or another, God is always at work within us to *will* and to *do* of His good pleasure (Philippians 2:13).

The word *dream* has two meanings. Obviously, it can apply to what happens while we sleep. Although some of those dreams can be divinely inspired, much of our dream life can be compared to taking out the mental trash. The word *dream* also refers to our imagination—to the *daydreams* of our hearts. Some Christians believe the imagination is sinful, and it is wrong to visualize this way. Yet almost every time Jesus begins a parable, He says, "Behold!" which basically means, "Imagine this!" So in Scripture, Jesus instructs people to use their human imaginations. God has given us the imagination to be able to envision what He desires to do in us and through us.

God Is a Dreamer

Out of all the awesome aspects of God, the most profound and overwhelming is His role as Creator. There is no greater revelation of who He is because we wouldn't exist without this one attribute. God's creativity includes concept and imagination before it becomes creation.

> In the beginning was the Word, and the Word was with God, and the Word was God. He was in the beginning with God. All things were made through Him, and without Him nothing was made that was made (John 1:1–3).

It is interesting that Scripture describes Jesus as the Word. Creativity is the process of moving from *concept* to *action*, and the bridge between the two is the spoken *word*.

A word is the verbalization of a concept or idea and is almost always the bridge between imagination and its application.

Before God spoke the words, "Let there be," there was an idea or a dream. In the very heart of God, He saw creation: what He wanted, His desires, His passion, His heart, what He would do. He then spoke and caused these things to happen. My point is that the whole notion of a creator denotes someone who *envisions* an outcome and is then able to marshal the necessary resources to see it to completion. Creation begins in the imagination.

Imagination is an element of creativity that exists within the heart of God. God can envision realities. He can envision a solar system, a galaxy, and a universe. He can envision individual planets. He can envision plants, creepy crawly things, and animals. God was also able to envision you and me before He created us.

We were made in the image of God; therefore, we should expect to follow in our Father's footsteps and, on a much smaller scale, do what He does.

Passion and Divine Jealousy

Throughout Scripture, God describes Himself as a jealous God. The word *zeal* and the word *jealous* are actually almost synonymous in Scripture. When Jesus says, "Zeal for the Lord's house has consumed Me," He is talking about jealousy — an inner passion, an almost painful love, for the purposes of God on the earth. This kind of zeal is a combination of imagination, aspiration, and passion.

Obviously, in the human construct, imagination left unbridled can turn into fantasy, daydream, a degree of hallucination, or even delusion. When imagination runs amuck, there can be all kinds of negative outcomes. In Romans 1, Paul writes that the people's imaginations were constantly toward evil; they were always envisioning new ways to do harm and difficulty.

However, when imagination is submitted to God, it becomes something very beautiful and powerful.

When we consider how we were made in His image, it only makes sense that we would imagine as God imagines, that we would dream as God dreams, and that we would aspire as God aspires. We can do these things because He can do these things. We can envision something, and what we envision, we can aspire to, and what we aspire to, we can generate a passion to see fulfilled. And what we passionately desire, we can begin to bring to pass.

Aspirations Versus Ambitions

As I talk about the relationship of dream to destiny, I am aware that much pain in the world has occurred as a result of unbridled imaginations, dreams, and selfish ambitions. But it is important to remember that there is a difference between a God-given yearning for something to come to pass and a selfish desire for a carnal purpose. I separate the two by calling the former *aspiration* and the latter *ambition*.

Ambition is the human drive to secure oneself in the realm of fame, fortune, and blessing. It is normally powered by fear, insecurity, and pride, and it is rooted in the unrestored human heart. When we are disconnected from God, our aspirations turn into selfish ambitions that are driven by fear, insecurity, and survival. This process perverted the original intent of godly aspiration and ultimately ended up producing war, poverty, heartache, broken families, and broken lives.

But on the other end of the spectrum is *aspiration*, which is driven by godly zeal and purpose. There is a passion in the heart of God for certain outcomes, and He has a boiling zeal to bring certain things to pass—He *wants* them to occur and "He watches over His word to perform it."

God wants us to be filled with passion and desire just as He is, but He wants those passions to be sanctified. The apostle James says that the fervent and effectual prayer of a righteous man "avails much"(James 5:16). Zeal and fervency are not only the key to Kingdom aspiration but also the key to sustaining a righteous life over a lifetime.

I believe that aspiration, imagination, and true spiritual passion come out of the highest part of who we are. They express the highest end of the human soul as it touches what we call "the spirit." And spirit, I believe, is the seat of godly imagination.

Aspiration is something we want to ignite in the heart of every person who is pursuing destiny in Christ. Each of us needs to understand, *I have a dream. I have a purpose in life, and I can aspire to fill that purpose. I don't have to feel useless. I don't have to feel unimportant. I have great desires in my heart, and God is going to help me see them come to pass!*

In Philippians 3:8-10, Paul writes, "I want to apprehend that for which Christ apprehended me." He wanted to lay hold of God's purpose for him. That desire propelled him forward; he called it his prize. "I press toward the mark for the prize of the high calling of God in Christ Jesus." Clearly, Paul's strength of passion was not sinful ambition. This was godly aspiration.

Created to Aspire

We were made to aspire. I believe God created us not just with creative impulse but also to rule and reign over our planet. He created us as stewards over giftings, abilities, and resources and gave us the ability to innovate and apply ingenuity to create things on the earth.

God made us to dream — to envision amazing possibilities and futures. He made us to create and innovate just as He does, and He wants to harness the power of desire and godly zeal in our lives.

Dreams and Passions in Scripture

The Bible is filled with the stories of men and women who aspired to great things and dreamed great dreams. Here are a few case studies that illustrate how dreams and passion can work toward destiny in a person's life.

Abraham

Abraham was a man who was already fairly accomplished when God first called him. He had flocks, herds, and servants, but he did not have a son. When God told him to leave his country and his father's house, the man didn't know exactly where he was headed, and God made it clear to him that He wasn't going to tell him.

Instead, He told him, "I'm going to bring you somewhere you have never been, and I am going to give you a son, and through your seed, all the nations of the earth will be blessed."

God gave him the seed of a dream very early on, but He didn't give him the capacity to fulfill that dream on his own. This propelled Abraham into a season of testing. He had to live in the tension of unfulfilled promise, and he ended up falling into different levels of failure and derailment. But after twenty-five years, the dream finally came to pass. His wife conceived even though she was past age, and they gave birth to a son.

In Abraham's story, we see God planting a passion inside a man; He gave him a promise, deep in his soul, and that promise ended up becoming a star in his life that guided him to a place of destiny and fulfillment.

Moses

As a tiny child, Moses was rescued off a raft from the waters of the Nile and raised in the house of Pharaoh's daughter. At some point, he became aware of the fact that he had Hebrew lineage. When he became a man, he saw a Hebrew being mistreated by an Egyptian. He was filled with rage and passion and killed the Egyptian.

Without approving of this act of violence, we can see in this story an unredeemed passion for his people that drove him to an extreme action. Moses killed a man in a broken response to an impulse that God had placed in his heart. Although he didn't know how to respond to the passion within him in a godly way, that passion was a precursor to all he was called to do.

He knew he had committed a capital crime and fled from Pharaoh. After forty years in the wilderness, he had an encounter with God in the burning bush, where God told him, "Now is the time to fulfill that dream. It is now time to lead My people into freedom."

David

The beginning of David's story suggests that he was the least of his brothers and was assigned some of the worst duties a brother could be given.

But in the midst of these things, he was a musician and worshipped the Lord. He took his shepherding job seriously and stood against the lion and the bear when they came to attack the flock in the wilderness. This all prepared him for a sense of promise he had to have felt in his life even from a young age — that he would be a great leader someday. A passion and a dream were growing inside of him, and they culminated in Samuel's anointing of him, his defeat of Goliath, his acclaim from the people, and his becoming king of Hebron and later of all Israel.

This young man had a dream of leadership. Initially, that leadership was just over a few sheep, but because of his faithfulness in small things, God later exalted him to be the leader and shepherd of His people.

Esther

Esther is another example of a biblical character who stepped into her calling and discovered her destiny. At a young age, she was taken from her home to be one of the king's concubines, ultimately auditioning for the role of queen.

Although she began her journey as a royal sex-slave, it is evident that she had a sense of the destiny on her life. Likely, this quality came through the leadership of her uncle, Mordecai, who had an obvious, strong sense of loyalty to God and his people.

Esther was selected to be the queen and was brought in

and purified according to the king's command. Although she could not fully understand what God was doing at every point, she knew she was representing her people and being positioned for possible impact in God's purposes.

When Haman, the king's advisor, made plans for Israel's destruction, Esther spoke with her uncle, learned of this plan, and worked with him to see the law abolished. Part of their counter-plan involved Esther herself coming before the king, at the risk of her own life, to intervene on behalf of her people.

Compelled by loyalty to her people and a sense of passion in her spirit, she was able to bring about a victorious outcome. Her uncle was exalted to a place of high leadership, while Haman was hung on the gallows that he had originally built for Mordecai.

In Esther's story, we see another example of an individual's sense of dream and destiny that upheld her in difficult circumstances and gave her courage to risk her life to save her people. She was truly brought into the kingdom "for such a time as this."

Mary

It is difficult for us to understand the courage it took for a young virgin to obey the Lord by conceiving a child out of wedlock and carrying that child to birth in such a religious culture. Yet Mary had received a promise from an angel that she would give birth to the Messiah. That promise brought forth a dream, and she walked out that dream with dignity and poise.

One part of this dream was fulfilled nine months later when the baby was born in the town of Bethlehem amidst the celebration of angels and the praise of poor shepherds.

The other part of the dream took thirty years to fulfill as this faithful mom raised a boy into a man and then released that man to change the world. Mary was the one who urged Jesus to turn water into wine. She was there for many of His miracles and teachings, but ultimately, her greatest and most painful moment was when she stood at the foot of the cross. As she watched the death of her son and the death of her dream, she couldn't know that three days later, she would see Him again, resurrected and victorious.

But when it happened and the dream was fulfilled, I am confident that Mary rejoiced over the blessings that would come to humanity and also over the blessing of a destiny fulfilled.

Paul

The apostle Paul had an amazing conversion experience, but even in his unconverted state, we can see the evidence of his true calling. He had a vision for truth, for what was right and wrong, for the health of God's people. Even though he was misguided, he was filled with a sense of passion that caused him to fight for truth, as he knew it. At the time, that meant imprisoning and persecuting these upstarts called Christians, who were ruining the Hebrew faith.

We find the story in his own words in Acts 26, when he shared his testimony with King Agrippa. On his way to Damascus, he had an encounter with Jesus that left him blind and dumbfounded.

Jesus said to him, "Why are you persecuting Me?"

Paul asked, "Who are You, Lord?"

"I am Jesus, whom you are persecuting. For this reason I have appeared to you, so you can turn people from darkness to light, from the dominion of Satan unto God, that they might receive the forgiveness of sins and the hope that is in Me."

At the end of the story, Paul told the king, "Wherefore, O king, I was not disobedient to the heavenly vision."

Paul was immediately launched into his destiny, and he never looked back. Although he may not have anticipated everything that would happen throughout his life, we know that he became the most impactful believer in his time—and throughout all time.

His ministry and writings have been used by God to bring a countless number of people out of darkness and into the glorious light of the Kingdom.

The Delight of God

Those are just a few of the stories of men and women who were chosen to fulfill a dream and a destiny. Although their stories are different from one another, they provide a picture of how God brings us from dream to destiny. This process can sometimes be a rollercoaster, but God is dedicated to making it happen. God delights in you and is committed to making you the person He has called you to be. One of the key ways He does this is by cultivating desires and dreams inside of you that match His will for your life.

King David put it this way: "Delight yourself also in the Lord, and He shall give you the desires of your heart" (Psalm 37:4). When I first read this, I assumed that meant

God would give me everything I desired. While I still believe that God wants to give me what I want, the true meaning of this passage is that *God shapes and directs* the desires of our hearts. So there is a molding process in which desire works in tandem with gifting and calling to create our ultimate expression of destiny.

The Delight of God's People

When we take religion at face value and try simply to fulfill our obligations, we become duty driven. This is never pleasing to the Lord. God never desired duty to be the primary foundation of His relationship with His people. Even as far back as Exodus 19, just before the Law was given to Moses, we find God expressing His desire for personal relationship, but the people were frightened of Him and rejected Him.

They told Moses, "You go talk to God. We don't want to talk to Him. It's too scary. You go meet with Him, then tell us what He says and we'll do it."

The people of God chose to distance themselves from the Lord in a way that made Him the arbiter of duties to fulfill and not the delight of their hearts. However, God's desire for us is that He would be our delight and that we would be His delight. David tapped into this in Psalm 27:4:

> One [thing] I have desired of the LORD,
> That will I seek:
> That I may dwell in the house of the LORD
> All the days of my life,
> To behold the beauty of the LORD,
> And to inquire in His temple.

David's passion was directed toward a real

relationship with God, and that passion for God culminated toward the call on his life to become a great leader, one who would usher in a golden age for his people.

That remains true for each of us: God is looking for hearts that delight in Him. When Jesus is asked, "What is the greatest commandment of all?" He replies, "You shall love the LORD your God with all your heart, with all your soul, and with all your mind. This is the first and great commandment. And the second is like it: You shall love your neighbor as yourself." Desire, delight, enjoyment, and undivided affection are the seat of all aspiration inside of us.

In Conclusion

Kingdom passions, dreams, and desires are important keys to understanding and fulfilling your personal destiny. They tell you a lot about who you are and what you are designed to do in life. Although your dreams and desires are not necessarily a precise indicator of destiny, they are a great "approximate" starting point in the discovery process. As your dreams are identified and combined with a clear understanding of your three dimensions of spiritual gifts, you have a great foundation for moving forward.

There are several helpful ways to begin to identify passions and dreams. Again, one way is to look at the things that bother you. Think of the global issues that trouble you the most or the social problems that cause you the greatest grief. Think about the things that bug you most about your church, your workplace, or your family. Often these dislikes are reverse indicators of what you are called to be and do. As you examine the things that bother you, ask the Lord what you can do to make a difference. Your Kingdom passions will begin to surface as you ask these questions and others like them.

Another way to identify your destiny is to look at the sphere of society to which you feel most attracted. You may have a desire to go into medicine or education. You may see yourself acting in a film or performing a song onstage. You may see yourself as a stay-at-home mom or dad, or you may see yourself traveling around the world as a representative of a relief agency. Give yourself permission to dream. Take time to journal your dreams and desires, and keep a record of the process of discovery you are going through.

It is also important to begin to think about your future scope of impact. As you think of yourself in your destiny role, consider whether you are most comfortable interacting on a one-on-one basis, in small groups, or overseeing larger groups of people. In addition to thinking about the number of people, it is also helpful to consider the kind of people you envision yourself working among. Think about race, age, ethnicity, and subcultural distinctives. Consider whether your work will be among a particular people group or whether it will be broad and inclusive.

TEN
Destiny Detours and Dead Ends

The destiny discovery process is a lot like taking a major road trip. Imagine yourself driving from San Francisco to New York. You have some choices for your route. You could get on I-80 and start going east. Or if your journey is in the winter, you may want to go south on I-5 and hook up with I-10 that goes across the warmer southern states; then, when you hit the East Coast, you can just turn north. On the other hand, if you're traveling in the summer, you may want to start out by heading to Seattle, and then you can go east on I-90, which is an amazing highway that takes you through a lot of scenic areas.

Here's the point: On the initial portion of your journey, it doesn't matter much which road you take as long as you are going in the right general direction. It is only after you have gone a good distance that you have to start thinking about how to approach your exact destination.

Specific directions are much more important at the end of the journey than they are at the beginning. The same thing is true with achieving your destiny. The older you get in life—the further along you are in this journey—

the more specific you need to be. As you get closer and closer to your destination, exactitude becomes increasingly important.

Even if you map out your journey perfectly, you may encounter a few detours along the way: roads closed, bridges washed out during floods, or snowstorms that make a road impassable for a season. It is also possible you will have a flat tire or need some engine work. There could be detours and difficulties during the destiny journey as well. Jesus promises us that in this world, we would have tribulation, but He also says, "Be of good cheer—I have overcome the world."

In our destiny development, there are numerous factors that can disrupt our journey, but they fall into two general categories: external and internal.

The external factors are the detours and difficulties that exist in the world around us. These can come in the form of people who hinder us, circumstances that confront us, and spiritual warfare that is designed by dark forces to derail us.

The internal factors, on the other hand, are the inner wounds and weaknesses that cause us to be vulnerable to the enemy's attacks. They also include areas of sinful thoughts and behaviors that sabotage destiny. These are the things Jesus is referring to when He says, "I will no longer talk much with you, for the ruler of this world is coming, and he has nothing in Me"(John 14:30). Here, Jesus is saying two things: The enemy wanted to trip Him up, but he had no access points in Jesus' life.

We Need to Keep Our Lives in Alignment

Let us take this journey metaphor in a different

direction. In a certain sense, each of us is like a vehicle. Some of us have been well maintained. Others of us have gone through different kinds of accidents and problems and are more vulnerable to breakdowns in the future. Each of us has to learn how we operate and how to keep ourselves in top condition so we can get to our individual destinations. We need to test out our brakes and keep all of our fluid levels topped off.

And just as it is with a car, we have to keep our lives in alignment; otherwise, we will wear out our tires to the point that they blow—sometimes taking out other vehicles at the same time. When our lives aren't aligned with Jesus, the enemy is thrilled.

In this chapter, we will be looking at five areas of the human soul that are vulnerable to the malfunctions that create opportunities for the enemy to sabotage us in our journeys:

- *Appetite* has to do with physical desires,
- *Affection* involves our emotion health,
- *Assumption* encompasses our mental makeup,
- *Attitude* has to do with the posture of our will, and
- *Aspiration* is the hope of the spirit.

If we have aligned each of these areas with God's purposes, we are good to go. If we haven't, we are vulnerable to the detours the enemy has set up along the way. If left unaddressed, these five areas can develop into "strongholds" of false beliefs and demonic attack, which then could create blockages to the fulfillment of destiny.

We will be going over each of these areas in this chapter. For additional information about them, visit www.destinyfinder.com, which contains a full evaluation of these areas, as well as areas of blockage that a person may have as a result.

Appetites:

God Created Our Desires But He Requires Restraint

Every one of us has a physical body that was designed by God to eat, drink, sleep, reproduce, and fulfill dozens of other functions that God ordained for us to fulfill. To sustain all these behaviors, God also gave us appetites such as hunger, thirst, and sexual desire that help us stay on track. Along with these desires, He also gave us the ability to manage our various hungers through the exercise of discipline and self-control.

Unfortunately, we live in a consumer society that is driven by commercial marketing. The success of marketers depends on their ability to play to our appetites. Obesity is one of the biggest problems in our country, and yet in spite of all the warnings, the problem continues to grow, especially among children. I find it interesting that so many people wait until they have a heart attack or some other severe situation to initiate a diet and exercise program. This is like waiting for your car's engine to melt down before you pay attention to your oil levels.

I understand how hard it is to exercise preemptive discipline — to take steps that create and maintain health within our bodies. But if we don't, the enemy could take advantage of us through disease and injury that might have been avoided had we learned to manage our appetites.

Just as God gave us appetites for food, He also gave us sexual appetites, which are to be managed and kept within appropriate boundaries. No doubt, you have heard people say, "Sex sells." But as a result of this truism, our culture has slid into an obsession with sex, and our consciences have grown hard and calloused. Those who allow themselves to feast on immorality are setting themselves up to be detoured in their destiny journeys.

When I was young, I used to get poison oak really severely, and one day while doing some yard work, I decided to get my revenge. In a moment of incredible stupidity, I decided to tackle a whole field of poison oak with my bare hands! As you may imagine, that didn't work out too well for me.

When people overindulge themselves in their appetites, it is just like rolling around in "poison oak." On the one hand, they cannot understand why their lives are tormented by lust and desires, yet on the other hand, they keep rolling in the same garbage that makes them itch every time. Whenever we do things like this, we don't realize that we are sabotaging ourselves, which tragically can keep us from fulfilling our destinies.

The apostle Paul was aware of the propensity of his body to hinder him on his journey and addresses this in 1 Corinthians 9:24: "Do you not know that those who run in a race all run, but one receives the prize? Run in such a way that you may obtain [it]." Think of Olympic athletes. They employ a great amount of discipline when they train for the gold. We, too, need to discipline ourselves for the race. Athletes who compete for the medal know how to control their appetites. They do so to obtain a perishable crown, but we do so to obtain an imperishable one!

Paul continues in verses 26–27:

> Therefore I run thus: not with uncertainty. Thus I fight: not as [one who] beats the air. But I discipline my body and bring [it] into subjection, lest, when I have preached to others, I myself should become disqualified.

Everything that brings us success in life requires practice and discipline. Practice makes perfect; it enables us to better ourselves and move forward. If we want something, we have to apply ourselves. Conquering the human appetites requires a degree of application — of diligence and the willingness to change.

This is one of the reasons fasting is so important. When we fast, we are preemptively limiting our appetites for the purpose of resetting our spiritual focus. Learning how to control appetites within ourselves prepares us to accomplish great things and withstand whatever challenges that may come.

Affections:

Emotions Are Good Servants But Bad Masters

Many of us are ruled by our feelings. Feelings are wonderful servants, but they are tyrannical masters! If you have not learned to master your feelings, you are incredibly vulnerable to the detours that the enemy uses to keep you from God's purposes in your life. Some of the enemy's favorite detouring emotions are fear, anger, resentment, rejection, and disappointment. Many people have limited themselves by getting trapped in these pits.

God made human emotions as a reflection of His emotions. This is one more way in which we are made in His image. He becomes grieved. He gets frustrated. He gets angry. He feels tenderness and love. God has emotions, but He isn't ruled by them. To move forward toward our goals, we must put off destructive emotions and put on the love of Christ.

Paul writes in Ephesians 4:26 that we can be angry, but in that anger, we should not sin. For me, the interesting thing about this passage is that Paul is quoting Psalm 4:4, which goes on to offer a solution: Be angry; do not sin, but *ponder* in your heart why you feel this way. Then process your anger before the Lord.

Many of us do not process our emotions effectively with God, and as a result, we .end up carrying our emotions inside of us. The emotional pressure eventually builds up within us to a point where we "blow up," get angry, or misbehave in some other way — because we have been carrying things that really should have been laid at Jesus' feet. We need to learn how to process our feelings with God.

How do we do this? Typically, as Psalm 4:4 suggests, it is a process of praying through the feeling. We pray about the emotion and bring it into alignment with Jesus. Consider Colossians 3:1–4:

> If then you were raised with Christ, seek those things which are above, where Christ is, sitting at the right hand of God. Set your mind on things above, not on things on the earth. For you died, and your life is hid with Christ in God. When Christ [who is] our life appears, then you also will appear with Him in glory.

In the King James Version of Scripture, the word *mind* is translated *affections.* Set your affections on things above and not on things of the earth. Pray through the emotion with God until you experience a sense of resolution. Then purposefully turn your thoughts away from the feeling, choosing to align yourself with Jesus with thanksgiving and praise.

Processing emotion with Heaven can also include venting your anger in the presence of God. *God, I'm really upset about this! This bothers me!* If you can't be honest with God, then you can't be honest at all. Hebrews 4:12 states:

> For the word of God [is] living and powerful, and sharper than any two-edged sword, piercing even to the division of soul and spirit, and of joints and marrow, and is a discerner of the thoughts and intents of the heart.

I think we need to allow God's presence and His Word to search us and reveal those areas where we are struggling.

King David was a master at opening his heart before the Lord. Many of the psalms are open expressions of emotional weakness and need, but almost every one concludes with a resolving statement of praise and restored trust in the Lord.

As a pastor for three decades, I can say that the majority of problems that people face result from unresolved emotion. If you are struggling with chronic sin or a pattern of broken behavior, chances are it is rooted in a dysfunction in this area.

Paul exhorts us in Colossians 3:8, "Put off all these: anger, wrath, malice, blasphemy, filthy language out of your mouth." Verse 12 offers the alternatives: "Therefore, as [the] elect of God, holy and beloved, put on tender mercies, kindness, humility, meekness, long-suffering." We are commanded to bring our affections into alignment with God, and we do this through our relationship with

Jesus.

In bringing our hearts into connection with Him, we find relational re-alignment. As a result of relational alignment, we have emotional alignment. And from that place of emotional alignment, our affections are submitted to our Creator and not to the destroyer.

Some people mistakenly assume that self-control and various types of self-discipline are "religious practices" and nothing more. They think, *'If you're forcing yourself to do certain things, you're being religious.'* But Scripture itself declares that self-control is one of the fruits of the Spirit.

So there is a godly form of self-discipline that we need to embrace in the area of appetites and affections. We cannot simply go around doing whatever we feel like because we are "in Jesus." That type of thinking becomes another form of self-centeredness, which is the very root of sin in our lives. We must be God-centered, not self-centered. Let us center our emotions in the Lord.

Assumptions:

Right Thinking Is Essential to Destiny Fulfillment

Assumptions are the fundamental beliefs we have about the world around us. They create a structure for how we perceive and process life. What we believe about God, ourselves, others, and our circumstances will determine our sense of well-being and our interactions with others in the workplace and every area of life.

Paul wrote in 2 Corinthians 10:3–5:

> For though we walk in the flesh, we do not war according to the flesh. For the weapons of our warfare

[are] not carnal but mighty in God for pulling down strongholds, casting down arguments and every high thing that exalts itself against the knowledge of God, bringing every thought into captivity to the obedience of Christ.

You and I are involved in a life-long spiritual battle, and the primary battlefield is not the heavens but our own minds. Our attitudes influence our beliefs, which in turn inform our thoughts and help us to interpret reality. So our assumptions become the foundation of false thinking; what we assume to be true about the universe becomes the building blocks of our beliefs. This is what the in 2 Corinthians passage calls "strongholds."

God tells us to be "transformed by the renewing of the minds" (Romans 12:2). The mind is very important to God. We are to love Him with all of our hearts, minds, souls, and strength. We typically forget the word *mind* in that verse because we more often think about loving Jesus with our hearts and souls. But we need to love Him with our minds as well. The mind is the realm where our assumptions determine our outcomes, and ultimately, our beliefs strongly influence our behaviors.

You and I are called by God — and are responsible before God — to bring our thoughts, assumptions, and ideas into alignment and agreement with what God thinks. That is our stewardship. What happens when we do not do this? We find ourselves with a stack of false assumptions, or strongholds.

Faulty beliefs and wrong assumptions can form *strongholds* in our minds. A stronghold is a "house" or structure of thought that is in conflict with God's truth. The term "stronghold" is an interesting one in Scripture. It does not refer to the "big picture" work of the enemy in the cosmos but to the finite picture of the enemy's influence on human thinking.

A cross reference for strongholds is found in Ephesians 4:26, where we are told to "not let the sun go down on your wrath, nor give place to the devil." Instead of "place," some translations say "foothold" or "stronghold." In other words, if believers allow wrath or anger into their hearts, and fail to process that anger quickly, they run the risk of developing a *stronghold* through which the enemy can then begin to influence their thoughts and behavior. Saved or unsaved, people can experience this. Obviously, if we are born again and follow the Word of God, we have an advantage over strongholds. However, even as Christians, we are vulnerable if we allow ourselves to come into agreement with darkness; the Book of Ephesians, after all, was written to believers.

As we can see, unresolved anger can become a stronghold of darkness in a person's life. Anger that remains unaddressed can turn into bitterness or resentment; a "root of bitterness that springs up will defile many" (Hebrews 12:15).

Fear can also be a stronghold. Those who have been raised in a violent or unstable world will often develop a stronghold of fear that can torment them throughout life. This can also happen as a result of trauma experienced later in life.

Some who have this stronghold of fear will try to overcome fear by *fight*: They become stronger, more assertive, and even rebellious. Others cope with fear by *flight*: They withdraw deep into themselves, detach from the world, and become hindered. Fear and insecurity can also lead to pride. This can produce an inordinate confidence in individuals, who may then assert themselves in an untoward manner. There can also be strongholds of lust, promiscuity, self-pity, and a myriad of other expressions that can hinder an individual from fulfilling his or her destiny in Christ.

The list is long and varied, but every stronghold sets itself up against the knowledge of God. Said another way, all strongholds are patterns of belief that are contrary to God's belief system. They are patterns that become frameworks, which then begin to control us.

The course of our lives is determined by the beliefs and behaviors that we have chosen, and those choices will either get us closer to God or further away from Him. This is why it is so important to identify our false assumptions, demolish mental strongholds, and bring every thought into obedience to Christ. We need to learn to recognize the patterns of broken thinking and repent for them.

Metanoia, the Greek word meaning "repentance," does not mean to "feel sorry." It means "to think differently." So in order to truly repent, we must begin to transform our thinking, adopt biblical beliefs, and confess biblical beliefs as our own. As we do this, we will begin to behave in a manner consistent with the new beliefs that God gives us. That is how strongholds are broken.

In any area where you have knowingly or unknowingly embraced a falsehood, you can follow Jesus' advice: "'know the truth, and the truth shall make you free" (John 8:32). Actually, it is not the truth that makes us free…it is the "truth that displaces the lie" that sets us free.

His truth displaces the lies: the wrong and often unquestioned assumptions that we have allowed to rule over us and keep us from fulfilling our destinies. Bring all assumptions into alignment with the truth of God.

Attitudes:

The Will Consists of Attitudes That Lead to Actions

You have likely heard the saying "Attitude is everything." It may not be *everything*, but it does affect everything.

Attitude is the foundation of the will and influences why and how we make the choices we make in life. However, I would distinguish here between *attitudes* and *emotions*. An attitude is not a feeling; it is a posture of heart that allows me to make right choices in the middle of difficult situations:

> Let this mind be in you which was also in Christ Jesus, who, being in the form of God, did not consider it robbery to be equal with God, but made Himself of no reputation, taking the form of a bondservant, [and] coming in the likeness of men. And being found in appearance as a man, He humbled Himself and became obedient to [the point of] death, even the death of the cross. Therefore God also has highly exalted Him and given Him the name which is above every name, that at the name of Jesus every knee should bow, of those in heaven, and of those on earth, and of those under the earth (Philippians 2:5–10).

The human will is the pivot point of life and is crucial to the process of fulfilling one's destiny. Subjecting your will to the will of God is one of the most important exercises that a believer can possibly do.

Jesus declared that it was His will to do the will of the Father, yet even Jesus struggled with this issue when He was in the garden. He sweat great drops of blood and prayed, "Father, if it is Your will, take this cup away from Me; nevertheless not My will, but Yours, be done" (Luke 22:42). As Jesus was going to the cross, He struggled; He interacted with the Father over the necessity of His death in this manner, but as soon as He knew the Father's will, He submitted and embraced it.

"Let this mind be in you," Paul writes. What kind of mind? He is referring to our attitude. What kind of attitude are we talking about? Through the Holy Spirit, the mind and attitude of Jesus Christ reside inside of us. Even though Jesus had it all, He gave it all up to do the Father's will. Because He gave up His will to do the Father's will, God highly exalted Him and made Him Lord. We, too, need to adopt this kind of full, complete submission to the Father's will.

What keeps us from submitting to God's will? Key hindrances would be heart attitudes such as rebellion, pride, despondency, and cynicism. Many of us maintain certain attitudes apart from God, and this polarization prevents us from being fully used by Him. Some of us are offended at Him because He didn't do things the way we thought He ought to. Some of us are offended at the Church, and as a result, we are hindered in our desire to be good members of the Body of Christ and share our gifts and receive the gifts of others. Because of these things, many become limited in their pursuits of destiny and purpose and resign themselves to fruitlessness as a way of life. Resignation is a horrible attitude. It is exemplified in this modern phrase: "Whatever."

God has a better purpose for us! He didn't die on the cross so we could give up. Let us align our wills with His will so our attitudes can align with this truth: "For it is God who works in you both to will and to do for His good pleasure" (Philippians 2:13).

If you are struggling in this area and are having a hard time bringing your will into alignment with God's will, take hope. As long as you keep returning to the Lord and resubmitting to His will, God is able to work inside of you to make you want the things that He wants for you.

Realignment gives God permission to work in us and through us. The more He works through us, the more our attitudes align with His and the more empowered we are to fulfill His purposes on the earth. That is a great cycle.

Aspirations:

Fostering Hope to Fulfill Our Destinies

The word *aspiration* is a synonym for *hope* and *dream*. In order to fulfill our dreams, we need to have our aspirations united with God's aspirations for us.

Many people are torn and tormented by their ambitions and aspirations. They long for a type of life that always seems to elude them. Yet God created us to aspire to great things. I believe the only way we can truly achieve the fulfillment of our aspirations is when we join our aspirations to the purposes of God.

The message of this book is that you were created to fulfill a powerful destiny, but many never discover and develop their full potential because they harbor aspirations that are contrary to God's aspirations for them. Others fail to lay hold of their destinies because their individual abilities to harness aspirations were damaged somewhere along the way. In either case, unfulfilled aspirations can damage the heart, destroy our hope, and demolish our dreams.

Hope is the foundation of our future. Hope is absolute confidence in something that hasn't yet come to pass. It is the positive expectation of future good; it is the seedbed of aspiration.

As we discussed in the dream and passion chapter, aspiration is different from ambition. Godly aspiration says, "God, I want what *You* have dreamed for me." Human ambition says, "I want what I want." Without Jesus, most of our dreams are self-centered. It is only when we take our dreams and submit them to Jesus Christ that we find that true aspirations begin to emerge.

The apostle Paul knew this struggle between human ambition and godly aspiration. Beginning in Philippians 3:5, he describes himself as the Hebrew of Hebrews, of the tribe of Benjamin, blameless concerning the law. But compared to knowing Jesus, he considers it all a pile of trash. "My human ambitions? Garbage." Look at the end of this passage in verses 7–10:

> But what things were gain to me, these I have counted loss for Christ. Yet indeed I also count all things loss for the excellence of the knowledge of Christ Jesus my Lord, for whom I have suffered the loss of all things, and count them as rubbish, that I may gain Christ and be found in Him, not having my own righteousness, which [is] from the law, but that which [is] through faith in Christ, the righteousness which is from God by faith; that I may know Him and the power of His resurrection, and the fellowship of His sufferings, being conformed to His death.

Allow God to sift your aspirations and dreams. Invite Him to match them up with the "excellence of the knowledge" of Him so that you can pursue them with purity.

Get Apprehended By God

At this point, it is probably becoming clear to you that pursuing your destiny is not a piece of cake. The process can be very challenging.

When the pursuit of your destiny gets rough, remind yourself of those who have gone before you — those who lay hold of their purposes in life. Write out these verses and hold fast to them when the way has become unclear:

> Not that I have already attained, or am already perfected; but I press on, that I may lay hold of that for which Christ Jesus has also laid hold of me. Brethren, I do not count myself to have apprehended; but one thing [I do], forgetting those things which are behind and reaching forward to those things which are ahead, I press toward the goal for the prize of the upward call of God in Christ Jesus (Philippians 3:12–14).

Let's take a moment and review each of these different areas of the human soul: Appetite is the realm of the body, affection is the realm of the heart, assumption is the realm of the mind, attitude is the realm of the will — and aspirations are the realm of the spirit. Jesus died for the whole person, every aspect of who we are. His goal is to bring every part of our souls under His loving rule and reign. With God, all these things are possible.

As we wrap up this chapter, I would like to suggest three ways that we can "apprehend that for which we are apprehended by God." Those areas are dedication, deliverance, and discipline.

Dedication: We Need a Fresh Encounter with the Cross of Jesus Christ

> Therefore we also, since we are surrounded by so great a cloud of witnesses, let us lay aside every weight, and the sin which so easily ensnares [us], and let us run with endurance the race that is set before us, looking unto Jesus, the author and finisher of [our] faith, who for the joy that was set before Him endured the cross, despising the shame, and has sat down at the right hand of the throne of God (Hebrews 12:1–2).

If you are to discover and fulfill the destiny that God has for you, you must begin that journey at the Cross. Nothing less than full dedication to Jesus Christ will do. Erase the blackboard, forget those things that lie behind, and re-engage those things for which you are here.

When Jesus died for you, you died. You no longer have the right to live for yourself; now you live for Him who died for you and rose again. Dedicate yourself to God by coming face to face with Him, receiving His forgiveness, and thanking Him for breaking the power of sin. When you do, you are given renewed access to the power of His Kingdom.

Deliverance: Reject Demonic Influence

Before we walked with Jesus, every one of us lived "according to the course of this world, according to the prince of the power of the air, the spirit that is now at work in the children of disobedience" (Ephesians 2:2). As a result, we all were "demonized" to one extent or another. When we received salvation, we moved from "darkness to light and from the dominion of Satan to God." Yet to the extent that we were unable or unwilling to turn away from broken beliefs and behaviors, we continued to permit demonic influence in our lives. One wise teacher has said, "Get rid of the garbage, and you'll get rid of the rats." Yet some of us never fully took out the trash, and as a result, the rats hung around.

It is time to deal with all the areas of your life that are stinking up your destiny. We can do this by confessing sin and receiving forgiveness, by inviting the Holy Spirit to fill every place that isn't saturated with Him, and finally by resisting the enemy in every area of belief and behavior (James 4:7). If you are still having difficulty getting free, then ask for prayer; join a home group and invite some accountability into your life. Do whatever you can to get the healing you need, and God will "lift you up."

Discipline: There Are No Shortcuts to Your Destiny

To win a race, you have to train. Discipline is about vigilance and perseverance. Be vigilant in preparation and strategy. Persevere by employing the tools of victory in Christ: things like renewing your mind, taking your thoughts captive to His obedience, seeking God, knowing who you are in Him, and being healed from past wounds.

Discipline is the way we build our muscles and endurance in preparation for the contest. Many believers reject discipline as a "religious" or artificial activity. But it is no more artificial than a football player lifting weights in the gym. While it is true that you will never see that player lifting weights in the middle of a football game, the work he does in the gym empowers him when he finally gets on the field.

As you do these things, you will find yourself moving

forward. We will talk more about endurance and building strength in the next chapter.

In Conclusion

With Christ, we can overcome all obstacles and difficulties that arise within these five fields of the human soul: appetites, affections, assumptions, attitudes, and aspirations.

In order to do this, we must first be willing to *dedicate* ourselves to the task at hand. We need to keep offering and presenting ourselves as living sacrifices to God. We need to keep going back to Him and rededicating ourselves to Him because we are ever going deeper in that dedication.

Second, we need to pursue deliverance. To whatever extent we have been infiltrated by wrong thinking, demonic strongholds, and perspectives of darkness, we need to repent and turn back to God, taking every thought captive to the obedience of Christ. Ultimately, that is the meaning of deliverance. In its most extreme sense, *deliverance* can mean casting a demon out of someone, but in a more minor, "everyday" sense, deliverance is the breaking of demonic thought structures that can hinder the process of destiny development and discovery.

Finally, we need to employ the power of discipline by training and preparing ourselves to fulfill the will of God. When we want something bad enough, we will be willing to make changes in our lifestyles and submit ourselves to a training process that will bring the desired results. In the next chapter, we will explore this subject in more detail.

Keep your eyes on Jesus, and run in such a way as to win the prize.

ELEVEN
Diligence and Discipline: Duty and Delight

My wife and I have been married for more than thirty years, with the vast majority of that time spent on the "mission field" of San Francisco. In spite of the many challenges of ministry, Diane and I have managed to build and raise an amazing family, with seven children and two grandchildren. We are so blessed by each one of them and by each other. Our marriage, family, and ministry are all a testimony to God's goodness and faithfulness in our lives.

In addition to the grace and goodness of God, the other factor that accounts for our family's blessing is the fact that we have been able to persevere through the challenges and difficulties that life has thrown our way. As with many families, our road has not always been an easy one.

Diane and I first met during an SOS San Francisco outreach in 1980. I was twenty-three at the time and had co-founded this ministry with a few friends the year before. SOS was responsible for mobilizing and training thousands of believers from dozens of churches and ministries to share their faith in the parks and on the streets of San Francisco. Once a year, we hosted a ten-day outreach that gathered people from all over the nation to join us in reaching our city. This is where I met my wife.

Diane was raised in southern California and joined a ministry called Youth With A Mission shortly after she began walking with the Lord. She had just returned home from a School of Evangelism outreach when she heard about our ministry and came to visit. I can remember the moment when I first saw her. I thought, *Wow, this is an amazing woman!* Not only was she beautiful, but she also clearly had a glow of God's anointing upon her.

At that point in my life, I wasn't involved in dating — I was a confirmed "bachelor 'til the rapture." But I was so struck by Diane in our first conversation that I thought, in her case; I just might make an exception.

That first night of outreach, we divided up into groups and spread out all around the city. About thirty of us headed to Castro Street to worship the Lord and invite His presence into this neighborhood. The Castro district of San Francisco is home to a large concentration of homosexuals and is known for its clubs and nightlife. I was raised in this part of town and was excited to represent Jesus in my old stomping grounds. Diane came as a part of our team.

In this specific area, we decided not to do any witnessing but spend our evening in worship and prayer. However, the Sisters of Perpetual Indulgence, a group of gay men dressed as nuns, decided that we had no business in the area. They emptied out the bars and led a host of inebriated men to surround us in protest. Without exaggeration, they brought *hundreds* of people to shout us off the street. They began to yell and scream, and some of them became violent. This continued for about an hour before the crowd began to disband. In the heat of the moment, Diane and I grabbed each other's hands as we walked back to the church that was hosting us. Although we met under some pretty unusual circumstances, we managed to survive the mob and had a proper "date" a few days later. The rest is history.

Marriage and Destiny

Diane has been such an amazing partner, not just as my wife and the mother of our children but also in the pursuit of destiny. She has been instrumental in helping me pursue my destiny just as I have tried to support her as she pursues hers. Marriage is a large component of destiny and calling. I believe the person you choose, or have chosen, to spend your life with will play an integral role in shaping your destiny. In fact, your choice of spouse could be the single most important destiny decision you make, other than your acceptance of Jesus.

However, it is important to remember that God is able to lead you into your calling regardless of whom you marry. As a pastor, I have known many believers who had married non-believers and thought that they would never be able to undo this mistake and fulfill their unique purposes in God. But this is just not true. Although I do not recommend being "unequally yoked," God is so big and He loves us so much that even a challenge like this can be overcome by His grace.

I have also known individuals who were divorced and thought they had permanently sabotaged their destinies. Although divorce is a terrible thing and harmful to children and the overall institution of the family, God is able to redeem even the most difficult situation and work all things together for good.

Good Things Come at a High Price

Marriage can be very challenging for even the most compatible couples, but it is worth it for dozens of reasons. For most people, the family is the foundation of identity and responsibility, and it will always be a primary element in the fulfillment of personal destiny.

Still, achieving "happily ever after" takes a little elbow grease, especially when you have been married for many years. You have to keep sowing into the relationship. You have to keep building, working toward one another, and resolving difficulties. For most of us, these are not natural tendencies; instead, they require the conscious decision to be diligent and disciplined.

Like I said earlier, our life has not always been easy. Raising seven children is a major feat by itself, requiring a tremendous amount of love and grace. Pioneering and pastoring a church in one of the most challenging cities on earth was also a major task. During these years, we experienced major trials on many different fronts and major spiritual warfare from the enemy's camp. We also experienced more than our share of the normal challenges of pastoral work. I think you get the picture.

Without grace-filled perseverance, endurance, diligence, and discipline, I am fairly confident we couldn't have made it this far. Destiny fulfillment is not for wimps. Although ultimately, all blessings come from God, most blessings come at a price. If we are unwilling to pay the price of preparation, process, and perseverance, we are unlikely to get the reward.

Diligence, Discipline, and Destiny

The discovery and development of our destinies will never happen without a sustained commitment to press through difficulties to achieve what God has promised.

Certain promises of God do not seem to come about except through diligent pursuit—through patience and *endurance*. Hebrews 6:12 urges us to "imitate those who through faith and patience inherit the promises." In other words, if we endure, we will inherit. The author of Hebrews states this again later in 10:36: "For you have need of endurance, so that after you have done the will of God, you may receive the promise."

Similarly, Paul suggests in 2 Timothy 2:3 that only through endurance and discipline do we see positive outcome: "You therefore must endure hardship as a good soldier of Jesus Christ." He then goes on to describe three different kinds of occupations that require endurance and diligence: the soldier, the athlete, and the farmer.

The soldier is encouraged not to "entangle himself with the affairs of this life, that he may please him who enlisted him as a soldier." One of the greatest keys to success is not keeping a great "To Do" list but rather a great "Not To Do" list. If we want to achieve our purposes in life, we must learn to say "No" to the things that will distract us. Our captain is Jesus, and as we keep in close communication with Him, we will learn how to dedicate ourselves to the mission at hand and achieve the victory.

The athlete "is not crowned unless he competes according to the rules." There are rules that govern every aspect of life. In Christ, we are not under the law, but as in the case of gravity, it is a good thing to have a healthy respect for the law. In every societal sphere, every earthly sphere, and every heavenly sphere, there are norms and "rules" that can be discerned and utilized to fulfill the destinies that God has given us. Playing according to the rules in a given sphere, whatever those rules are is the key to fruitfulness and fulfillment.

Finally, the farmer "must be first to partake of the crops." This final example illustrates another dimension of the diligence and discipline question. Being a successful farmer requires an ability to plow, sow, reap, and store your crops successfully. It also requires wisdom to know how much of the harvest to keep back to feed your family and how much to plant again for the next harvest. The farmer needs to be disciplined, but he must also be able to enjoy the journey along the way. It requires a different kind of discipline to be able to rest, relax, and celebrate your blessings.

Pursuit and Perseverance

The pursuit of destiny is like a marriage—it is for richer or poorer, in sickness or health, and 'til death do us part.

Everyone who chooses to pursue his or her callings and destinies will be tested in the process. The forces of darkness are aware of God's purposes. They know that if you come into your fullness, their days are numbered. Therefore they will use every trick in the book to hinder you and discourage you in your pursuit. Thankfully, Jesus is infinitely more powerful than the enemy, and He is our shield and strength.

But even greater than the obstacles the enemy will

throw at us are the challenges presented by our own hearts. The greatest problem I have seen as I coach people in destiny discovery is that of self-sabotage. Ultimately, the only person who can keep you from discovering and fulfilling your calling is yourself. This is another reason *community* is so important. None of us can see ourselves or know ourselves perfectly. We need trustworthy truth-tellers to shine a light on our blind spots and shortcomings and help us move forward.

I do not think there is anything outside of us that can hinder us if our hearts stay close to Jesus and we remain filled with His grace, walking in obedience to His will.

Developing Your Destiny

You may look at your life right now and feel like you are so far from where you want to be. If this is the case, take heart. There is always hope.

As I told you before, I had a vision of the Lord before I really committed my life fully to Jesus. He asked me, "Are you ready yet?"

I did a quick inventory of my life and saw all of the things I was doing that were contrary to what I perceived God's will to be. I realized, *there is no way in the world I am ready…yet.*

Yet is one of the most powerful words in the English language. It says, *I may not be where I am going to be, but I am going to be there someday. I may not have the resources I need, but someday I am going to have them. God, the promise hasn't happened yet, but I believe it's on its way.*

Yet is also a powerful word in the destiny process.

The apostle Peter had his fair share of obstacles to

overcome before he could fulfill his destiny. Peter's main obstacle was his big mouth, and he also had a real problem with the fear of man. How did Jesus mold Peter into a man of God whose faith still impacts the world today? It took diligence and discipline applied over a long period of time.

To illustrate this, I would like to take a hard look at the life of the apostle Peter. When Peter started his journey, he was working in the family business—catching fish in a village by the Sea of Galilee. Jesus called him, saying, "Follow Me and I will make you a fisher of men." Peter took the risk, and no doubt, people thought he was crazy for doing it, but he persisted.

Right away, his personal issues began to surface. It seems like every other time Peter talked with Jesus, he said something ridiculous. As we talked about in an earlier chapter, at one point, Jesus asked His disciples, "Who do you think I am?"

Peter answered brilliantly: "You are the Christ, the Son of the living God."

This response showed great revelation and insight, and Jesus commended him because he heard from the Father. However, just a few minutes later, Jesus rebuked Peter as he tried to discourage Him from going to the cross.

Another example of Peter's unique issues was his propensity to quarrel with the other disciples about which of them was the greatest; and let us not forget what Peter did when he was on the Mount of Transfiguration with Jesus. When Peter saw Him transformed, he responded, "Jesus, it's great that we are here with You, Elijah, and Moses. Let us pitch some tents so we can stay here for a little while longer..." He totally missed what God was doing in the moment.

Before the crucifixion, Jesus spoke to Peter and declared, "Satan has demanded to sift you like wheat. But I have prayed for you, and when you are converted, strengthen the brethren." This prophecy foretold Peter's most famous failure: the denial of Christ. He did this not once but *three* times. Yet before His ascension, Jesus took time to encourage Peter, saying, "If you love Me, feed My sheep and tend My lambs."

Peter had inner problems and outer problems, but he was diligent and he persevered to the end. He kept on keeping on, and God honored his perseverance. Near the end of his life, he shared some valuable wisdom in his letters that encouraged the next generation to pursue their destinies.

Peter was a man who tried to take shortcuts and sometimes opted for the easy way out. But by the end of his life, we find a man of proven character, calling the Church to a level of virtue that is quite different from how fragile and unstable he used to be. Church history tells us that the Romans crucified Peter upside-down because he refused to do anything that would take away from the death of his Lord Jesus. Peter is a great example of God's ability to transform even the most unstable person.

In this moment, God is molding men and women in His image. As much as God wants to use us to do great things in life, He is far more concerned with *who we are* than *what we do*. As with Peter, God allows circumstances to sift us so that He can convert or transform us within. His work in us is most clearly seen in the way we process the circumstances of life: trials, temptations, disappointments, and pain.

Changed from Within

Peter is a great example of a spiritual "rags to riches" story. But the riches he gained were not material, nor were they measured in terms of his accomplishments. The true riches that Peter found were displayed in the transformation of his character into the image of Christ.

In the first chapter of his second epistle, Peter declares,

> ...His divine power has given to us all things that [pertain] to life and godliness, through the knowledge of Him who called us by glory and virtue, by which have been given to us exceedingly great and precious promises, that through these you may be partakers of the divine nature, having escaped the corruption [that is] in the world through lust.

Peter urges us to remember that God's Spirit dwells within us. We have access to the transformational power needed to become the people God has called each of us to be. He has already called us—past tense. This is a done deal! We have been given all these things.

Peter goes on to say that he has escaped the corruption that is in the world through lust. The lust he is referring to is not merely sexual lust; it is covetousness, idolatry, and the longing for a life other than the one you have.

Happiness is not about getting what you want—it is about wanting what you've got. If you trust the sovereignty of God and believe He is over your life, then you have to believe that every step of the journey, even your missed steps, are covered by Him and His goodness.

God has given you all the equipment you need, so don't covet what someone else has, whether that be looks, intelligence, financial blessing, or whatever else. If you can't be happy *now*, you won't be happy when or if you get what you think you want. Be careful to guard your heart against the lust that brings corruption:

> For this very reason, giving all diligence, add to your faith virtue, to virtue knowledge, to knowledge self-control, to self-control perseverance, to perseverance godliness (2 Peter 1:5-6).

Peter builds on this in verse 10: "Therefore, brethren, be even more diligent." Diligence requires us to concentrate, to be focused on a certain goal.

Diligence and discipline are not convenient. We are called to swim against the tide. And in order to become the people God has called us to be, we must actively partner with His purposes, and this requires intentionality.

Diligence gives us the prescription and power for transformation.

Add Virtue to Faith

Peter goes on to say, "With all diligence, add to your faith virtue." Each one of us comes to Jesus by faith. Faith alone saves, but the faith that saves is not alone; we have to add *virtue* to our faith. That means we have to activate our consciences and our lifestyles to reflect the goodness of Jesus.

God has given each of us a conscience to help us determine our course in life. We need to be able to tune our consciences to what the Scriptures say is right and wrong. Then we will begin to live in a virtuous manner.

Add Knowledge to Virtue

Next, we need to add knowledge to virtue. In the same way that faith must manifest itself in virtuous belief and behavior, we need to add *knowledge* to expand the scope of virtue.

Hosea 4:6 clearly tells us, "People are destroyed for lack of knowledge." We need to grow continually in the knowledge of God as 2 Timothy 2:15 instructs: "Be diligent to present yourself approved to God, a worker who does not need to be ashamed, rightly dividing the word of truth."

Add Self-control to Knowledge

Peter continues his thought by encouraging us to add self-control to knowledge. Some Christians I know have detoured because they were unwilling to master themselves and their emotions. Remember that emotions are a great servant but a terrible master! If you put your emotions in the driver's seat of your life, you aren't going to go very far.

Faith is the foundation for virtue, and virtue is the foundation for expanded knowledge. Faith, virtue, and knowledge together empower a life of self-control and keep it from becoming a duty-driven religious ritual.

A multitude of benefits can be found in a life of self-control and moderation. We feel much better when we eat healthy foods, engage in physical exercise, and maintain good sleep habits. We are more spiritually healthy when we are consistent in prayer, fellowship, and the other disciplines of the faith.

Self-control is a powerful thing. The Proverbs say that

if a man can master his own heart, he can rule a city. God wants to give us cities, and he is waiting to entrust them to us as we demonstrate our trustworthiness.

Add Perseverance to Self-control

When I was a new believer, I remember meeting an older Christian who had been serving the Lord for five years, and I was floored. How did he do it? What was his secret? It was hard for me to comprehend that anyone could maintain any kind of commitment for that length of time. But as I write these words thirty-five years later, I rejoice at the way I have grown in my understanding and appreciation of perseverance.

What is perseverance? It is the ability to hang in there over the long haul. Perseverance is in the same family of virtues as longsuffering and endurance. Most people can control themselves for short periods of time, but exercising faith, virtue, knowledge, and self-control over the course of months and years requires perseverance. Ultimately, the prize belongs to those who endure. Destiny fulfillment is not a sprint but a marathon.

The reason Diane and I were able to minister in San Francisco for more than thirty years is very simple: We refused to quit. God is raising up an army of sons and daughters who are dedicated to His purposes and unwilling to relent until He receives the full reward of His sufferings. God's grace is able to strengthen our resolve and empower us to serve in increasing strength into the future.

Add Godliness to Perseverance

Godliness is the manifestation of the character of Jesus. The thread that runs through faith, virtue, knowledge, self-control, and perseverance ultimately ends in godliness—so in other words, it ends when our nature matches the nature and character of Jesus.

> For whom He foreknew, He also predestined [to be] conformed to the image of His Son, that He might be the firstborn among many brethren (Romans 8:29).

As we allow Him to cultivate His character within us, we begin to display brotherly kindness and love. What God works within us eventually comes out of us and touches other people's lives in a powerful way.

In 2 Peter 1:8, Peter writes, "For if these things are yours and abound, [you] will be neither barren nor unfruitful in the knowledge of our Lord Jesus Christ." In other words, fruitfulness is the result of the nature and character of Jesus manifest within us.

Godly character is essential to true destiny fulfillment. Gifted people are a dime a dozen. God has made all of us amazing, but the ones who bring the most glory to Him are the ones whose gifts and passions are firmly rooted in the soil of Christ-like character and demonstrate the qualities of Jesus throughout their entire lives. The result is the testimony of one who has "finished well."

Spiritual Disciplines

Throughout history, the majority of men and women who have changed the world were those who understood the power of spiritual disciplines. In recent years, teachers like Dallas Willard and Richard Foster have worked to renew our appreciation for the historic disciplines of the faith.

Unfortunately, many people misunderstand and misapply the disciplines as well as undervalue the benefits offered by discipline and self-control. My hope in this chapter is to encourage us to learn the value of discipline in the pursuit of destiny.

As I have said earlier, self-control is a fruit of the Holy Spirit, and it has immeasurable value. One of the key benefits of spiritual disciplines is what I call the "self-induced trial." When we exercise Spirit-led disciplines, we create a "controlled trial" that can work in us to accelerate spiritual growth.

James tells us to "count it all joy when we fall into various trials" because trials that are processed correctly produce godly character. In a similar way, spiritual disciplines, when practiced correctly, can produce the same result as a trial that comes in the normal course of life.

When I fast, give a generous offering, witness to a friend even though I don't feel like it, or do something else out of discipline, I am inducing behavioral change and generating the same inner friction that God would use to bring transformation in a normal trial.

I affirm the fact that the Spirit-filled life is most effectively lived out of delight rather than duty. I also recognize that discipline, by itself, can lead to religious legalism that can be very harmful to a spiritual life. Still, it would be a serious mistake to throw out the baby with the bathwater. Disciplines can enhance our spiritual growth when they are used wisely.

Peter ends this section with a severe statement: "For he who lacks these qualities is shortsighted, even to blindness, and has forgotten that he was cleansed from his old sins" (2 Peter 1:9).

Let us diligently live the Christian life with eyes wide open to the finished work of Christ and our individual destinies within that work.

Three Keys to Unlock Destiny

We finish this section with 2 Peter 1:10–11:

> Therefore, brethren, be even more diligent to make your call and election sure, for if you do these things you will never stumble; for so an entrance will be supplied to you abundantly into the everlasting kingdom of our Lord and Savior Jesus Christ.

When Peter says, "Make your calling and election sure," he is essentially saying, "God has called you to a higher purpose, and along the way, you are going to accomplish great things for Him. But you have a responsibility to partner with God to bring it to pass."

We can help make our calling and election sure by growing in information, skills, and personal character transformation.

Grow in Information (2 Timothy 2:15)

To pursue our destinies, we need to grow in knowledge and information—to inform ourselves. This means we need to grow in our knowledge of the Scriptures, of the history of the Church, and of those who have gone before us. It also means that we need to grow in knowledge that is relevant to the spheres to which God has called us. God desires that we raise the standard of excellence in all we do. This depends on our ability to remain life-long learners.

Skill Formation (2 Timothy 2:1–7)

To achieve our destinies, we must also develop the skills necessary to serve Jesus in this earth, according to the destiny call on each of our lives. These skills include life skills, discipleship skills, and ministry skills. But they also include the professional skills to ensure our influence and impact within the various spheres to which God has called us.

Character Transformation (2 Corinthians 5:17–24)

Finally, we must pursue character transformation to fulfill the call of God. Transformation begins at the Cross, but it extends throughout our lives. When we give our lives to Jesus, we are born again and we become new creations in Christ. This shift in identity is the first step in character transformation. Then follows the life-long process of incremental change.

God is dedicated to transforming you into the image of His Son. So whenever you get stuck in any area, remember the Cross. As John Wimber used to say, the way in is the way on. Jesus declared, "It is finished," and His transforming power is at work within you.

> But we all, with unveiled face, beholding as in a mirror the glory of the Lord, are being transformed into the same image from glory to glory, just as by the Spirit of the Lord (2 Corinthians 3:18).

Avoid Leveling Off

Discipline and diligence are best maintained when you are motivated. Paul was motivated and stayed motivated through his life. He was a tremendously focused individual. Motivation is how we win the race. When my motivation is to glorify Jesus, everything else finds its right context, and I have the ability to sustain the pursuit of my destiny through any trial and circumstance.

When a jet reaches its desired altitude, it levels off until the end of the flight. Paul never leveled off. He kept climbing and climbing, growing and growing, moving and moving—all because he was rightly motivated. Like Paul, we have the ability to keep climbing and never peak. When you feel yourself beginning to "level off," go before the throne of grace and have your fire reignited.

Every believer is called to be a leader in one way or another. As a leader, it is essential that you stay motivated so that you can motivate those you lead. The greatest motivation for the people you are leading is the treasure you help them discover within themselves. That treasure—their destinies—is for the glorification of God.

When you remain motivated by Jesus' glory, you will motivate others from that place. Motivating people out of guilt and shame never works for very long. We need to mature and move beyond those things; God has given us much better motivating tools than guilt, shame, rejection, and fear.

When Jesus chose His apostles, they had all kinds of issues. They had problems of ego, identity, comparison and competition, insecurity, etc. But if we search the Scriptures, we never find Jesus motivating the apostles by punishing them for their problems or wrong motivations. Through the process of walking with Him for several years, the apostles became strong leaders of the faith who did amazing miracles among the people.

Motivation must be clean and pure; the truest motivation is inspiration. And the truest inspiration comes as we see that God's best is our best and that He is worthy of our living our lives to glorify Him.

Keys to Running the Race

If we are rightly motivated, what is the next step? In 1 Corinthians 9:24–27, Paul provides us with a few keys to running this race well. He begins with this thought: "Do you not know that those who run in a race all run, but one receives the prize? Run in such a way that you may obtain [it]."

The Prize: Keep Your Eyes on It

Martin Luther King Jr. used the Gospel phrase "Keep your eyes on the prize." King is a great example of someone who was able to follow his own advice. He was not a perfect man, but he loved Jesus and taught the Word with great power. He was also able to mobilize a movement of people—a people who changed a nation with their sincerity and passion to bring about justice through non-violent civil disobedience. One of the most impactful men of the twentieth century, King kept his eyes on the prize even to the point of his own assassination.

Studies have shown that humans are motivated by glory, reward, and significance. A reward, or *prize*, is not an inherently evil motivation. In fact, it is the primary way

God motivates His people. He used reward in Scripture, and He continues to use it today.

Our prize is the pleasure of God and the fulfillment of God's will in our lives. Nothing can ultimately compare to the motivation that comes from the hope of hearing these famous words, "Well done, good and faithful servant. Enter into the rest of your Lord."

Though we look forward to that final affirmation, we are also running to win today. If we are running just to show up at the end, I think there is something wrong with our motivation. I want to be the best that I can possibly be for Jesus. He is my prize.

The Pace: Be Temperate in All Things

And everyone who competes [for the prize] is temperate in all things. Now they [do it] to obtain a perishable crown, but we [for] an imperishable [crown]. Therefore I run thus: not with uncertainty. Thus I fight: not as [one who] beats the air (verses 25–26).

We need to pace ourselves. As I mentioned earlier, this life is a marathon; it is not a sprint. When I was a new believer, I came sprinting off the blocks. I ran hard and fast for almost a decade and then slammed into a few brick walls. Those walls took the wind out of me, and while I was catching my breath, issues that I hadn't dealt with began to surface from the depths of my heart. I found myself going through years of processing and healing to unseat issues that I thought I had already moved beyond.

Marathon runners do get off the blocks pretty fast, but they hit a stride that they can maintain for twenty-six miles and still finish strong. We need to be like that. We want to finish well, but we don't want to burn out along the way. Let us pace ourselves to finish well.

The Price: Practice, Practice, Practice

> But I discipline my body and bring [it] into subjection, lest, when I have preached to others, I myself should become disqualified (verse 27).

There is a price for winning a race. That price is the many unseen hours of practice to build your speed, your strength, and your aerobic capacity. When the race finally comes, you can win it because of the hundreds of hours you spent preparing for it.

In this life, we are running for an eternal crown. It is worth sacrificing for, and it is even worth limiting ourselves for. Do not level off. Keep pressing, learning, growing. Keep receiving God's grace. Limit yourself from the pleasures that would level you off in this life. They may be good, even godly, pleasures, but you know that they are a distraction and not a provocation to greatness. "He is no fool who gives up what he cannot keep to gain what he can never lose." Those are the famous words of Jim Elliot, who gave his life in pursuit of a small tribe in the Amazon. His wife, Elisabeth Elliot, carried on his legacy and became a great author and missionary.

To gain what we cannot lose requires Spirit-filled willpower. This inner strength—in combination with great friends and mentors to help us stay motivated, diligent, and disciplined—will empower us to run the race set before us as we keep our eyes on the prize. That is why mentors are integral to the sustained pursuit of destiny. We will discuss the importance of mentors in the next chapter.

In conclusion, if we want this—if we want to see the destinies God has planned for us pan out in our lives—we need to be willing to work for them. Yes, the destiny journey is fun, exhilarating, and exciting. Sometimes it can even be easy. But it is important for us to remember that the destiny journey is a *vocation*, not a *vacation*. It requires discipline and diligence. Keep your eyes on your goal, be temperate in all things, and remember that practice makes perfect. This journey in God is fully worth the sacrifice.

TWELVE
Mentoring and Connection

In 1992, while ministering in Germany, Diane and I had an opportunity to visit the famous "storybook" castle called Neuschwanstein. This is the building that the Disneyland Castle was patterned after, with grand turrets and circular spires. My favorite part of the tour was seeing the ornate throne room. Its floor, walls, and ceiling were covered with over a million little tiles that formed a massive mosaic of creation. The floor portrayed the earth. The walls depicted the realm of men, and the upper walls and ceiling displayed the heavens in all their glory. Each little piece was a broken tile that had no recognizable shape or form. By themselves these pieces were nothing, but when they were placed together by the hands of a master craftsman, they became one of the most amazing works of art I have ever seen.

This mosaic is an amazing illustration of the Body of Christ. Each one of us individually has a unique shape and color, but without our connection to one another, the picture is incomplete. When the Master Craftsman places us in relationship to one another, a picture begins to form of the One who is called the Desire of the Nations: the Lord Jesus Christ.

Individuality and Community

One of the greatest revelations I have received as a pastor is that *we were created for community*. We have talked about the importance of unity and community in previous chapters, but as we focus specifically on the topic of mentoring, I want to reiterate that although our salvation is entirely personal and individual, God created us to walk out that salvation in relationship, fellowship, and a life of *interdependency* with others.

This concept of community was difficult for me to grasp because I was a bit of a loner in my teenage years. From childhood, I learned to fend for myself and intentionally cultivated a strong independent streak. As I told you earlier, when I was about fifteen years old, I began to travel around North America several months out of every year, and most of that time, I was alone. I learned to be self-sufficient and self-contained. I didn't really feel a need for anyone in my life. By the end of my teenage years, all I wanted to do was buy some land, grow my own food, and live apart from the pain and confusion of the world.

However, when I gave my life to Jesus and began to look at Scripture, I realized that God never intended for people to live in seclusion and separation — He intended us to live in unity and community with one another. Early in my faith, I was drawn to the Book of Ephesians, and I began to discover that community was not an afterthought but a primary focus of the plan of God.

Destiny discovery and fulfillment depend on our ability to balance individuality and community. God's plan is not simply about *you* — it is about *us*.

We looked at Ephesians 2:10 at the very beginning of

this book: "We are the workmanship of God, created in Christ Jesus for good works." But then in verses 19-20, Paul says:

> Now, therefore, you are no longer strangers and foreigners, but fellow citizens with the saints and members of the household of God, having been built on the foundation of the apostles and prophets, Jesus Christ Himself being the chief corner[stone].

So in the course of one chapter, we find the celebration of individuality and the celebration of community. Each one of us is a distinct *individual*, uniquely designed and gifted by God, but we are saved into a heavenly *household*, or a Kingdom family, called the Church. This theme of family is repeated in the next chapter when Paul prays to the Father "from whom the whole family in heaven and on earth is named" (Ephesians 3:15).

Clearly, God loves the family unit. In fact, we find the original expression of individuality in community presented in the Trinity. Although the concept of the Trinity is challenging for mere humans to understand, one thing remains crystal clear: God loves *unity in diversity*.

Destiny in the Family of God

I used to believe that God invented the family as a convenient structure to help humans live out their existence on earth. I didn't realize that family existed in the heart of God long before the first human child was ever born. The family that exists on earth is a reflection of the family that has existed forever in eternity, not the other way around.

When God created humanity, He could have given us

the ability to bring forth offspring who were fully grown and mature, but He didn't. Instead, He created a family structure in which a mother and father join their lives, and a child is conceived. This child grows from microscopic cells into an infant, who comes forth from the womb completely dependent and absolutely immature.

Similarly, Paul writes in 2 Corinthians 5:17 that "if anyone [is] in Christ, [he is] a new creation; old things have passed away; behold, all things have become new." We begin in immaturity—as infants and newborns in Christ—and grow to maturity through the love and nurturing of spiritual "parents." Just as our natural parents mentor us into positions of capability and understanding in the physical world, so our spiritual parents mentor us into positions of authority and influence in this realm of destiny.

Two thousand years ago, God began a work to transform the entire earth by transforming the hearts of just a few men and women. These new-creation individuals went and made disciples, and those disciples went and made disciples, and the process continued through the ages until today. The spiritual descendants of those original disciples, we join into clusters, congregations, and teams in which individuality expresses itself in diversified community. From these communities, Jesus selects and sends us out, commissioning *us* to go out into the world and turn it upside down.

We have inherited Jesus' commission to change the world by going forth and making disciples. Individually, we can each carry out a small part of this commission, but together, we can carry transformation throughout the earth.

Spiritual Coaching

I can't imagine a greater privilege than to have lived in the time of Jesus and to have walked with Him and learned from Him while He was on the earth. Yet Jesus says, "It is to your advantage that I go away; for if I do not go away, the Helper will not come to you; but if I depart, I will send Him to you" (John 16:7).

In this statement, Jesus reveals God's purpose in community and therefore in destiny. The plan of God was to send Jesus as the prototype of the new creation. While He lived on the earth in a finite body, Jesus was limited; however, when He ascended to Heaven, the Holy Spirit was poured out, and the new creation came to life. The Spirit of Jesus now dwells in each of us — we each possess a *portion* of Jesus. Like the mosaic in the castle, or the prism we discussed in Chapter Five, we each have a unique shape and color, but only when we join together can we display a deep, rich, multicolored image of His glory in the earth.

As we grow in community, we help one another discover how we are oriented and what gifts function most naturally in our lives. Not only does community display God's glory, but it also enriches and *empowers* us to fulfill our destinies. I believe that no one can fully know who he or she is apart from community. We all have blind spots and assumptions that limit our ability to see ourselves clearly. Yet in healthy relationship with one another, we can grow in our self-awareness and our ability to move forward. Jesus wants to be displayed by His people on earth. This happens when each of us brings our individual gifts and abilities and joins them to the gifts and abilities of others. God created us for *interdependency*.

We need to surround ourselves with spiritual brothers, sisters, mothers, and fathers who will "speak the truth in love" and help us become the persons God has called us to become. Speaking the truth in love is the key to strengthening each other's weaknesses and affirming each other's gifts and callings. Throughout Scripture, we see a pattern of mature men and women coming alongside younger, emerging leaders to help guide them through the challenges of life as they grew into the leaders God had called them to be. This is what we now call mentoring, or coaching.

Everyone Needs a Coach

When we think of great athletes or people who have made momentous accomplishments, we often discover that somewhere in their lives, each one had a mentor. For example, Barry Bonds was one of the greatest hitters that baseball has ever seen. He was able to hit the ball out of the park into the San Francisco Bay many, many times because of the strength and power of his swing.

But few of us remember that Bonds had a batting coach. I couldn't even tell you what that coach's name was, and I doubt that the coach ever played in the Big Leagues himself, but he drew the best out of the best player.

Coaches who have never played at a high level are often better teachers than natural hitters. Natural hitters hit from the gift within them, and they rarely understand what it takes from a scientific standpoint to get that ball out of the park. What a natural hitter knows is this: When his or her eye connects with that ball and there is power in the swing, something amazing happens. "It felt right," most of them often say.

Yet with all the talent in the world, even the best hitters go through seasons of slumps. Sometimes, what gets them out of that slump is a simple correction suggested by a coach, such as identifying the need to raise the bat a quarter of an inch or keep his or her head in. It took such coaching for Bonds to be one of the greatest home-run hitters of all time. He realized that an outside perspective was essential to helping him become the best he could be. The way Bonds hit the ball may have "felt great," but to be the best of the best, he knew he had to trust someone else more than he trusted himself. In the Kingdom, this is an essential principle that applies in every occupation and to every aspect of life.

With the emergence of the modern "life-coaching movement," there is a growing distinction between the role of a coach and that of a mentor. According to Tony Stoltzfus, my friend and neighbor and also one of the premier leaders in the coaching world, a coach is someone who draws wisdom and purpose out of you, while a mentor is someone who instills wisdom and purpose into you. A mentor is specifically trained to give you the counsel you need—in other words, his or her counsel is specific to who you are. A coach, on the other hand, can provide access to wisdom without having to know your specialty.

Although this redefinition of coaching and mentoring may not completely apply in the sports world, it provides a helpful distinction in the realm of personal growth. I believe each of us needs both types of people: someone to pour into us and someone to draw out of us so each of us can become the best expression of who we are designed to be. But regardless of how we use the terminology of *coach* and *mentor*, the basic role is the same: We need people outside of ourselves to help us grow and achieve our highest potential. It is too easy to convince ourselves that we are something we are not or to think we are more mature than we are. We all struggle with some level of self-deception. A leader can help objectify our self-perception and clarify our life purposes.

Overcoming the Orphan Spirit

One of the biggest obstacles to our discovering and fulfilling our God-given destinies is what many are calling the "orphan spirit."

Most of us who grew up in recent generations had a physically or emotionally absent father. As a result, we have had to make our own way in the world. We haven't known how to draw from the maturity and wealth of wisdom that our fathers possessed. Instead, we have had to fend for ourselves.

But as we try to figure out and do everything on our own, we develop negative patterns in our lives and embrace a competitive attitude toward our fathers. That attitude drives us to prove our value to them by trying to gain success independent from their success. We may or may not realize that we do this to gain their approval; we may or may not realize that this competitive heart can wedge animosity into our relationships, and, therefore, it needs to be addressed.

Much of the division and strife that has occurred in the Body of Christ over the years has been because of insecure, orphaned leaders rising up under insecure, orphaned fathers. This creates cycles of division and strife in the body, as well as attitudes of rebellion and orphanhood. In order to remove this brokenness from the Church, God is raising up spiritual fathers and mothers and joining them to spiritual sons and daughters to help them move from a place of immaturity to maturity.

Turning the Hearts of the Fathers

In the final words of the Old Testament, God declares:

"Behold, I will send you Elijah the prophet
Before the coming of the great and dreadful day of the
LORD. And he will turn the hearts of the fathers to the
children, And the hearts of the children to their fathers,
Lest I come and strike the earth with a curse" (Malachi
4:5–6).

There is a curse of fatherlessness that exists on the earth today. We find the results of this curse in every sin and problem on our planet. We see this curse displayed in countless dysfunctional families, broken homes, and broken lives. Yet it is important to remember that this curse is not a vindictive response of an angry God, afflicting humanity in His wrath. The curse is merely the consequence of a generation responding to the absence of true fathers and mothers; subsequently, the corruption of godly authority has released brokenness on the earth. This is the very brokenness we are trying to heal and correct by understanding and pursuing true destiny.

We need to become leaders who are secure in our authority and who are able to raise up others into the fullness of what they are called to be. Those of us who are older need to embrace the emerging leaders around us and help them become a generation of men and women with excellent character, powerful gifting, and effective ministry to others. We are called to make our ceiling their floor and to help them come into greatness. They in turn need to do the same for the generation that follows them.

Depending on where we are in the process of our own destinies, we may or may not *feel* like spiritual parents, but in some way, shape, or form, all of us are called to spiritual parenting—to love, nurture, mentor, raise up, and send out specific people whom God brings into our lives. We show them the Father by example and by teaching, and they in turn go out and show the Father to others.

As spiritual fathers and mothers, we need to turn our hearts toward the daughters and sons around us and call them into their destinies. Our specific manner and "style" of mentoring may look different based on our specific callings and unique gift-mixes, but the key is to look for the gold that is buried within other people, whether they see it in themselves or not. We need to learn how to confront with love, speak into their lives, and bring the Word of the Lord to them. Mentoring includes putting them in positions of responsibility that will allow them to test, perfect, and refine their gifts, yet all the while we stay connected to them and nurture them as they grow.

John Wimber had a simple system of developing new leaders and mentoring them. He boiled it down to "identify, recruit, train, deploy, monitor, and nurture." That six-part system is the basic function of leadership development and mentoring.

Ultimately, God is restoring true spiritual parenthood in our day and age so that His spirit of adoption will counteract the spirit of orphanhood and release people into their full potential in Christ.

God Leads Through Spiritual Leaders

God is the universal mentor and eternal life-coach who delegates His leadership and Fatherhood to men and women whom He has ordained to lead His people. He has prepared and gifted these leaders to provide catalytic influence in the lives of aspiring believers. As I said before, the Great Commission is a universal mandate for all believers, but different leaders with different gifts carry it out in different ways.

One of the most important roles of a mentor is to help the disciple set reasonable growth goals and then help him or her fulfill them. Goals are essential to spiritual growth. As the saying goes, "If you aim at nothing, you are certain to hit it." A skilled leader is able to help a person discover his or her dreams and identify measurable steps to accomplishing those dreams. The leader is then able to provide support and counsel as these steps are taken and the dream is ultimately fulfilled.

Culture of Honor

Much of the fulfillment of destiny depends on the leaders functioning well in the body, and in that, it is important to understand the difference between *leadership* and *fatherhood*. In 1 Corinthians 4:15, Paul explains:

> For though you might have ten thousand instructors in Christ, yet [you do] not [have] many fathers; for in Christ Jesus I have begotten you through the Gospel.

That is part of the apostolic gift—it is a fathering gift. The apostle Paul considered himself a father not only to certain congregations but to certain individuals as well. He often referred to Timothy, Titus, and others as "sons." We also find Paul instructing Timothy to be a father to others: "And the things that you have heard from me among many witnesses, commit these to faithful men who will be able to teach others also" (2 Timothy 2:2). In this verse, we have four generations of leadership delegation and spiritual fatherhood: Paul delegated to Timothy, who delegated to faithful men, who delegated to others.

Implicit in this leadership flow is what many would call a "culture of honor." Danny Silk, in his amazing book *The Culture of Honor*, provides a framework for cultivating and empowering relationships in the family of God. He writes that honor is essential to maintaining a good mentoring relationship because it provides an environment of mutual respect and trust.

Many leaders demand respect and honor but often fail to give the same to their subordinates. The culture of honor recognizes the Spirit of God in every person and bestows "honor to whom honor is due." The mentor is worthy of honor because of his or her maturity, experience, and expertise. The apprentice is worthy of honor for his or her aspirations, gifts, and potential.

For the delegation cycle to be complete, we extend honor to those we are leading, entrusting them with something that is valuable to us, showing them that we are empowering them to take care of what they have been given, and releasing them to empower others with honor and respect. If we do not lead through honor and respect, we will raise up and send out people who have no respect for authority, and they will end up producing division and strife. They will inevitably draw people to themselves instead of to a vision of Jesus.

The Responsibility Lies with the Apprentice

As you begin to prepare yourself to enlist a mentor or coach, it is important to remember that just because the person is older and more experienced doesn't mean he or she is perfect. All of us have weaknesses and difficulties in our own lives, and we need to be able to see beyond those things to the maturity and wisdom that God has given that particular person. We need to position ourselves in alignment with our leaders in a way that enables us to draw the maximum resource from them for our own transformation. Said another way, in order for mentoring to work, the right kind of submission is needed. This is not a blind obedience but recognition of God's authority working in and through our mentors.

Taking this one step further, I believe that the responsibility of mentoring should always be on the apprentice and not on the mentor. If the responsibility is on the mentor, then the apprentice often feels un-chosen and un-fathered, whereas if the burden of apprenticeship is on the apprentice, he or she will take responsibility in the mentoring process. The one being mentored can then access a mentoring "grace" from not just one mentor but from an entire constellation of mentors, many of whom may not even be aware that they are being used to help. In other words, when I accept responsibility for the mentoring process, I can draw mentoring understanding from people without formalizing that relationship by calling them my mentors.

I have had the privilege of walking with a number of amazing spiritual leaders throughout my years of ministry. Some of them may have names you recognize, and some may not. Some have been fathers and mothers for me, and some have been mentors and coaches, but all of them have left a significant deposit in my life.

My fruitfulness is a product of the input of many awesome individuals. I am indebted to the dozens of mentors, living and dead, who have influenced my thinking and actions over the thirty-five years of my ministry. All of those individuals have had a role in imprinting my destiny and shaping my life message. They called out my destiny, and the older I become, the more I realize that I can do no less for the people around me.

THIRTEEN
A Call to Fruitfulness

When I was interning as a gardener, half of my internship was spent landscaping, and half was spent vegetable gardening. After launching my own business, one of my initial projects was to oversee a garden that was half ornamental, half vegetable. One fruit tree in the garden had not borne fruit for several years. I decided to tackle the challenge. Instead of cutting it down in order to plant something that would produce fruit, I dug around the roots, fertilized the tree, took off the diseased areas, and pruned it back significantly. Then I waited. As winter turned into spring, I joyfully saw the branches caked with blossoms. Within a short period of time, the blossoms fell away and little buds of fruit began to grow.

That tree yielded a great harvest, but this harvest did not happen all on its own. The work that was put into the tree in order to make it ready is what caused it to bear fruit. If I had decided to cut it down instead of cultivate it or just leave it to be fruitless for yet another season, I would not have experienced the joy of seeing the buds turn to blossoms and the blossoms turn to fruit.

Fruitfulness and Fulfillment

As I think about that fruit tree, I think about the amazing call of God on each of our lives to bear fruit. One of the very first things that God said to Adam and Eve after He made them in the garden was, "Be fruitful and multiply." Obviously, God was speaking of filling the earth with offspring, but He was also giving an indicator of His will for every area of our lives. The original definition of "fruitfulness" was to raise up a generation who raises up a generation who raises up a generation. This cycle was designed to continue throughout history until the earth is filled with the object of God's desire: human beings. Every new generation and every new individual produces an amazing myriad of options and opportunities, of potential and promise.

As each generation gives birth to the next, the earth becomes filled, not with robotic clones but with thousands upon thousands of variations of humanity — all of them created under the loving eyes of God to fulfill individual destinies that He has ordained for each one. That is a second definition of fruitfulness: the fulfillment of destiny.

Centuries after God commanded Adam to be fruitful, God made a promise to a man named Abraham, saying, "Blessing I will bless you, and multiplying I will multiply your descendants" (Genesis 22:17). Blessing and multiplication are the two dimensions of quality and quantity in the Kingdom of God. God wants to *bless* us by enriching the quality of our lives. He also wants to *multiply* us by adding to the "quantity" of our lives, and this means fruitfulness.

As I have said throughout this book, we were each

created to fulfill a God-given destiny. Our ultimate destiny is to live with God forever in Heaven, but our individual destinies begin now as we fulfill God's purpose on Earth.

I do not believe that when we get to Heaven, our own individual destinies stop. In Heaven, I believe that we will live through an unfolding of eternal destinies. We will not be bound by time or hindered by sin the way we are now. Instead, we will work out those destinies in a place of growth, creativity, beauty, wonder, relationship, and love.

For now, while we are here on this earth, we have a brief opportunity to take what God has invested within us and use it for His glory. In this chapter, I want to talk about a spiritual principle that is mirrored in the natural: Fruitfulness comes from intimacy. Said another way, if you want to be fruitful in your destiny, you need to need to be connected to the Father.

The Vine and Branches

In the Upper Room discourse in John 15, Jesus declares Himself to be a vine and His followers the branches. The implication of a vine and branches is that they exist for one thing: fruit. You don't dine on the grape leaves, and without the possibility of fruit, you wouldn't use the branches for anything other than a field fire. The whole purpose of the vine is to bear fruit. Jesus says, "I am the true vine, and My Father is the vinedresser" (John 15:1). God deals with us in a way that nurtures our greatest fruitfulness on the vine. He is working with us, pruning us, fertilizing us, digging around our roots, and helping us to become the people He has called us to be.

God has said that if we abide in Him, if we have

intimate relationship with Him, and if the very thoughts of His heart are living inside of us, then we will bear fruit, and we will demonstrate the fact that we are His disciples. "If anyone does not abide in Me," He says, "he is cast out as a branch and is withered; and they gather them and throw [them] into the fire." If we don't abide in Him, we won't bear fruit, and if we don't bear fruit, we will be cut away. I don't believe this is talking about Hell but rather the consequences of fruitlessness in this life.

All of us are called to be productive and successful, and to the extent that we are these things, we enter into fruitfulness and fulfillment. To the extent that we are not, we find lives of futility and frustration. God is working inside of us to cultivate faithfulness so that we can be fruitful, with the ultimate goal of being fulfilled and seeing Jesus get His full reward. Later in the John 15 passage, Jesus says, "These things I have spoken to you, that My joy may remain in you, and [that] your joy may be full" (John 15:11). In other words, our "fruit production" is a matter of happiness and delight, not merely labor.

Leadership and Fruitfulness

In this process of fruitfulness and fulfillment, God has given us a spiritual family—a community of people who can support us, as we read in 1 Corinthians 12–14 and Romans 12. Why is community so important in this context? We are designed to bear fruit alongside of one another and share our fruit with one another—to supply things that no one else can supply. We have been joined together by God to have a symbiotic relationship with one another whereby each of us supplies a different aspect of God's heart. Clearly, this cannot be done apart from community. Ephesians 4:16 tells us that His Body is "joined and knit together by what every joint supplies, according to the effective working by which every part does its share, causing growth of the body for the edifying of itself in love."

And into this body God has placed leadership. We have looked at leadership as those who pull out the full potential of every individual. Essentially, this is for the purpose of helping people bear fruit and be productive. As a friend of mine says, "Accountability is not about making sure you don't smoke. It's about making sure you burn." Leadership focuses on bearing fruit!

True leadership is not about managing the flock, keeping everybody in line, or making sure they don't sin. In other words, it is not about sin management. True leadership is about pulling forth the gold in everyone and believing in people before they deserve it. Leadership calls out the treasure hidden in the hearts of each man and woman and equips them to make the highest impact possible in the world around them.

The Lordship of Jesus is unlike any other example of leadership. Jesus cultivated fruitfulness in everyone He interacted with and in the community that He developed. The goal of His leadership was fully aimed at fruitfulness for the Kingdom. Jesus says that we will be held accountable for the fruit we bear. This isn't said in an angry way—He is not waiting for us to mess up so He can punish us. Rather, Jesus is saying, "You were created for one thing: My Father's glory. And this is My Father glorified: that you bear much fruit."

The Three Kinds of Branches

In every destiny, occupation, leadership position, and relationship, Jesus is the source of true fruitfulness. Having a deep, intimate relationship with Him is the way to fruitfulness. He declares (paraphrased), "If you abide in Me and My words abide in you, you shall bear much fruit."

In human biology, fruitfulness comes from intimacy. The same is true in the Spirit. Intimacy is defined as "a close, familiar, and affectionate personal relationship with another person." With God, it is not merely about praying or praising, but it is also about listening and responding. Intimacy is about a life of continuous interaction between our hearts and the heart of God. I cannot stress this enough: Intimacy with God is the source of all fruitfulness and fulfillment in life. If you want to succeed in your destiny, get your priorities straight.

I have sought to maintain a good prayer life through my Christian walk, and I have made it my aim to maintain the depth of intimacy in which His words are constantly abiding in me, where they are living inside of me, and I am living inside of Him. The Father is always tending to my relationship with Jesus and keeping intimacy alive and growing, keeping me in the highest posture of fruit-bearing that is possible. As I grow in new directions, I extend my branches, allowing the buds to form and the fruit to grow and eventually be harvested.

If we want a good harvest, we need to be healthy branches. John 15 categorizes the branches into three distinct groups: fruitful, fruitless, and non-abiding. Understanding these three groups will help us see how the pursuit of destiny functions. Keep in mind, however, that changes can be made at any point. If you realize that your walk with God, and therefore your pursuit of destiny, is not where you want it to be, you can make changes at any time. The door to greater intimacy with God is open for you in every moment.

The Fruitful Branches

The fruitful branches are the people who live in deep intimacy with God, and as a result of this deep relationship, they impact and influence the world around them. This kind of fruitfulness is not to be confused with the fruit of human effort. Certainly, human beings are capable of great things as a result of natural wisdom and strength, yet Jesus made it clear that He was committed to doing only what He saw His Father doing. In John 15, He says specifically, "Apart from Me you can do nothing."

Sadly, much of what is called "ministry" today is simply what human beings can do in the power of human ability. God created each of us with a mind, emotions, a will, and a creative spark that is irrevocable according to Scripture, so even if we have cut ourselves off from Him, creative sparks and ingenuity still flow. However, the results of human effort will not bear supernatural fruit—such fruit only grows out of intimacy with God. When that intimacy is established, fruit can be born.

There is something to keep in mind about the branch that bears fruit—it is in a constant state of pruning. Our "Father prunes it so that it may bear more fruit." In other words, we may be doing really, really well, and still God may choose to cut us back. He is working with us; He is refining us; He is transforming us. In the end, His pruning means we can bear even more good-quality fruit.

The pruning of God is never pleasant, but as any gardener knows, if you fail to prune the branches well, you will fail to get a good harvest in the following season. Essentially, if you fail to prune the rose bush effectively, you won't have a good harvest of roses. Even when the branches are bearing fruit, sometimes the immature fruit needs to be thinned so that the nutrients will not be spread among a thousand apples but concentrated among five hundred; those five hundred apples have a better chance of being big and juicy because five hundred others were removed. In the same way, God will often "narrow" our focus of service so that we can concentrate our efforts and do a few things with excellence rather than a thousand things inadequately.

The whole pruning process is one of intentionality. God is intentional toward us; He chastens us for our own good, and He is calling us to be intentional in the process as well. When God is pruning us, we have a choice to *intentionally embrace* the pruning or to resist it. So in this destiny journey, when you find yourself being "pruned," it is important not to get angry and blame God. He is pruning you only because He loves you and desires your highest good. Whom the Lord loves, He chastens. This isn't punishment—this is a process of refinement of discipline. Scripture clearly states that as a good and loving Father, God disciplines His children.

Discipline is not the same as punishment. God is not an egotist who is trying to satisfy His own anger toward us by seeking revenge and inflicting pain. He is a loving Father who wants us to be as healthy and as fruitful as we can possibly be in Him.

The Fruitless Branches

Fruitless branches appear to be attached to the vine, but they do not bear fruit. Something happened at the connection point.

In a similar way, we can go to church, sit in the pews, attend home groups — but be connected with the Lord only at the base level of intimacy. The result is that we do not see much, if any, fruit in our lives.

Over the years, I have pastored thousands of people. One of the challenges I have experienced is that a fair percentage of them were so focused on their own pain, their own issues, or their own encounters with God that they never produced much fruit. They never volunteered, they never served, they never blessed others, but they were always at the next conference and in the next prayer line to receive something from the Lord. I am not opposed to people receiving as much as they possibly can from Jesus, but nutrients need to flow in *and* out of our lives.

We don't want to be the Dead Sea — a sea that has water flowing into it but doesn't have water flowing out. The result is a sea filled with stagnant and bitter water. We want to be like *rivers*; we need to be constantly flowing with the grace of God. The stream that comes into us from the Holy Spirit needs to be equaled by the stream that flows out from us. Again, the fruitless branch appears to be attached to the vine, but it never bears the fruit that God ordained for it.

With any type of fruitfulness, the basic place to begin is to serve where you can — to see a need and fill it.

The Non-abiding Branches

God is efficient, effective, and economical. The non-abiding branches are the ones that He has cut away and gathered for the smoky fire in the middle of the vineyard.

We know that God loves every person. When He cuts away the non-abiding branches, He is not negating His love; He is merely allowing the consequences of our choices to run their course. If we are drawing from God but are not giving back to God—that is, if we are Christians in name but are not pursuing Him and growing in intimacy with Him—we have created an imbalance. That imbalance will cause us to dry and wither.

These three kinds of branches are essentially the three kinds of Christians. Based on this analogy that Jesus presents in John 15, we can see that we need to be moving into deeper and deeper intimacy with God and to be living in ever-increasing intentionality with others. Let us look a bit further at the kind of branch we want to be: a fruitful branch.

How to Be a Fruitful Branch

In the Parable of the Sower, Jesus tells us that the sower went out to sow and tossed his seed on four kinds of soils. The first one was the trampled soil—the pathways in between the garden beds. It was so compacted that the seed could not penetrate it, and the birds of the air came and swallowed the seed up and took it away.

Many people have been trampled to the point that they cannot receive the Word, and they are cut off from hope, goodness, grace, and love. They have walled themselves off so deeply because of their pain, shame, and sinfulness that the seed cannot grow in the "trampled" places.

The second kind of soil is the rocky soil. In this case, the seed is able to grow a little bit in the pockets of soil between the rocks, but when the roots hit the impenetrable stone, the plants dry up in the hot sun. Similar to the trampled soil, these people are affected by unresolved pain in their lives, but the pain is like big areas of "rock" buried under the surface of their hearts. They do well for a season, but as soon as the Word of God hits those rocks, the work of the Word dries up because of unprocessed pain, self-pity, victimization, or unforgiveness. These individuals often appear to be growing, but when harvest time comes, they bear no fruit. They never allowed the Lord full access to their hearts, and so their hearts have never been fully cleansed from the pain, shame, guilt, or bitterness embedded there.

The third kind of soil is the weedy soil that received God's seed but also received many other kinds of seeds: the cares and pleasures of this world. These are seeds of distractions, and not all of them are necessarily "evil" distractions. Some of them, in the right proportion and proper priority, are perfectly legitimate "cares and pleasures." However, when our priorities are skewed, we run the risk of falling into idolatry.

The heart that is filled with the weeds of this world will work against the Kingdom fruit we are called to produce. In this case, the fulfillment of destiny becomes choked out by the other plants that are growing in our lives, such as entertainment, the arts, sports, hobbies, health, etc. These are all good things, but they need to find their rightful place under the purpose of God.

In addition to these good things that can become distracting weeds in our lives, there are also the negative things that should be completely avoided. As an obvious example, the sins and temptations that are spoken about in the Ten Commandments will certainly kill the seeds of the Gospel in our lives.

As a former gardener, I understand how soil works. We had a tool called a cultivator that looked like a big fork with a ninety-degree bend in it. I could weed a garden, but if I didn't *cultivate* it on a regular basis, it would not stay weed free. The cultivator turned the topsoil just a little bit, exposing the weed seeds to light, which caused them to dry up and die. If I did that effectively, pretty soon there would be no more weed seeds in that garden, and the amount of care required after a year of careful cultivation became minimal. The same result can happen in our hearts.

The fourth kind of soil is the "good and honest heart" that Jesus describes in this parable. This soil receives the Word gladly, and the seed grows up to produce a harvest—some hundredfold, some sixty, some thirty. As I mentioned earlier, according to Jesus the human heart has some level of goodness in it, and it is open to receiving God's Word. A good and honest heart is not a *sinless* heart but a *seeking* heart; it is a heart that wants truth more than it wants to be right. It wants goodness and love, even though it doesn't have the ability to bring them about in its natural strength. Obviously, the human heart is sinful as a result of the Fall, but Scripture seems to suggest that as long as the heart is seeking, it is capable of a measure of goodness.

A good heart is one that will look upon the innocent

and want to defend them; it will look upon the injured and want to comfort them. The good and honest heart receives the Word and grows the Word until it bears the fruit of the Word: some hundredfold, some sixty, some thirty. This is the "branch" that abides in the vine.

In the Parable of the Sower, we see different levels of harvest. The difference of harvest is determined by the degree to which we give ourselves to God. When the hindrances caused by the rocks and weeds are removed, we become one-hundredfold believers.

God is moving us from a place of fruitlessness to a place of fruitfulness. A major hindrance to fruitfulness is the problem of self-reliance. The simple secret to discovering and fulfilling our destinies is to become "God reliant."

There is no greater way to grow in reliance upon God than to seek to live and minister in the supernatural power of the Holy Spirit. Many of the rituals and daily actions of Christianity can be accomplished in human strength, but the supernatural is something we can never fake. The supernatural—the realm of the impossible—depends on the presence and power of God working in the people of God. If we accomplish only what is humanly possible, the quality of our reliance upon God is never tested. But as we give ourselves to living in the supernatural by taking risks to share the Gospel, pray for the sick, heal the brokenhearted, and raise the dead, we will find that our dependence on the Lord increases incrementally and so does the fruit we bear for Him.

Ensure Your Fruitfulness

There are three primary ways to ensure our fruitfulness in the Lord.

First of all, we must continue to deepen our prayer lives. Some people say, "Well, I don't have a prayer time. I just pray all day long." Why not do both—a continual life of prayer *and* a dedicated time of prayer? We need focused prayer, and we also need consistent, continuous communion. Smith Wigglesworth said it well: "I don't often spend more than half an hour in prayer at one time, but I never go more than half an hour without praying." Fruitfulness is birthed in intimacy—in constant, daily communion.

The second thing is letting God's Word abide in us through memorization and meditation. Some people feel that if they can hear God's voice, they don't need to study the Bible, but that does not make sense to me. We do not serve a schizophrenic God. He is not going to say something to us in this day and age that He hasn't been saying to humanity for thousands of years. Jesus is the same yesterday, today, and forever. When we fail to have His eternal Word abiding in us, we will always be limited in our ability to hear His immediate Word.

We are instructed to study the Word, to meditate upon it. The Book of Psalms opens by saying:

Blessed [is] the man
Who walks not in the counsel of the ungodly,
Nor stands in the path of sinners,
Nor sits in the seat of the scornful;
But his delight [is] in the law (the Word) of the LORD,
And in His law he meditates day and night.
He shall be like a tree

Planted by the rivers of water,
That brings forth its fruit in its season,
Whose leaf also shall not wither;
And whatever he does shall prosper (Psalm 1:1-3).

Finally, we also need to obey the Word that we are hearing. In John 14:15, Jesus says, "If you love Me, you will keep My commandments." Charles Finny said that revival is nothing more than a restoration of obedience to the Lord. Obedience is not easy, but it is the truest form of worship in existence. It is also the purest form of alignment that we can ever enjoy with God.

Many of us are *performance driven*, and we obey out of shame and fear. However, shame and fear are poor motivators and only lead to legalistic religion. The obedience that God desires is one that is borne out of a heart of love. Obedience is *alignment*. It is the alignment of our lives with God in such a way that every single thing we do is a reflection of the transformed mind responding to the life-giving Word. As Bill Johnson tells the story, when Jesus asked His disciples if they were going to leave Him, they responded, "Where else can we go? When You speak, we come alive."

The Rewards of Fruitfulness

What is the reward of fruitfulness? The first reward is that our Father is glorified. "By this My Father is glorified, that you bear much fruit." (John 15:8). The fulfillment of our existence is in His glorification and honor.

The Father is honored when Kingdom passions displace selfish desires. He is glorified when the gifts He has given us are used to bless others and transform nations. As long as we keep our hearts in purity and keep the glory of God as our sole desire, God is honored by our lives bearing the fruit of love. And that is ultimately what destiny is: an expression of love for God and for others.

A second reward of fruitfulness is the personal fulfillment that comes as we glorify our Father. "These things I have spoken to you, that My joy may remain in you, and [that] your joy may be full" (John 15:11). Said another way, we become fulfilled as we fulfill God's purposes. Great pleasure comes from knowing that we give Jesus joy in the process of pursuing destiny. When we live in alignment with Him, our lives are filled with joy and blessing, and that deep sense of well-being manifests itself in joy unspeakable and glory to God.

Third, as we partner with God in our destinies, our friendship with Jesus becomes mature; we learn to be partners with the Holy Spirit. We join the "family business" — no longer slaves, we are friends and the beloved, intimate members of God's household.

Jesus says that a servant obeys but fails to understand why. But a friend, on the other hand, knows what the Father is doing and partners with God for the outcome. Servanthood is a good foundation for relationship with God, but our goal is *friendship*.

God is inviting each of us to move from servants to friends, to step into a place of partnership in His purposes.

The Stages of Destiny

Destiny almost always unfolds in stages, and each stage is filled with its own lessons, challenges, achievements, and promotions. It is similar to going to school. We begin in elementary school and have our circle of friends from first grade to sixth. But after sixth-grade graduation, we have to start over in middle school, where we are the new kids on the block. After a year or two there, we graduate and move on to high school and eventually college, where the process essentially begins all over again.

As we wrap up the subject of fruitfulness, I would like to review the seasons and stages of my destiny to help you further understand the seasons and stages of your own. But as you look at these points in my journey, I want you to notice a couple of things: First, God led me into different areas of service to teach me different things about who He is and who I am in Him.

Next, I want you to see that in each stage, I was doing very similar things according to my Destiny Orientation. I am a builder, and I am always seeing the big-picture vision of God and mobilizing others to help me fulfill that vision. Whether I am leading people in outreach or building a church, I will usually be doing these kinds of things.

The third thing I would like you to see is that each stage has a season of fruitfulness that is generally associated with graduation and promotion to the next level.

I began ministry in 1977 as an intern in a church planting team that moved to San Francisco to pioneer a new church in the city. We began house ministries, established businesses, launched home groups and a Sunday service, and cared for hundreds of people over the course of the next six years.

During that time, I co-founded a citywide outreach ministry that united churches and believers to share the love of Jesus in the parks and streets of San Francisco.

During this stage of my destiny, I helped unite dozens of churches, train hundreds of believers to share their faith, and touch thousands of people with the Gospel of the Kingdom.

In 1984, my wife and I started a new church with four people that grew to be one of the largest churches our city had seen in a generation. The Vineyard of San Francisco was born in revival and enjoyed fifteen years of fruitful impact in the Bay Area. We trained hundreds of people to become leaders and to minister in the supernatural. We pioneered many small groups and ministries. We baptized hundreds of new believers and brought healing and deliverance to many.

After several years, I was asked to serve as a Vineyard district overseer for northern California. We helped plant over a dozen churches and eventually supervised over twenty-five churches. We were also privileged to host another major outpouring of the Holy Spirit in the mid-1990's in which we were able to minister to thousands of people from all over the Bay Area with physical and inner healing and deliverance, providing opportunities for life-changing encounters with God.

In 2000, after a series of difficulties and challenges, our church dropped from almost a thousand people to around a hundred, and we started over as a new congregation called Promised Land Fellowship. For the next ten years, I continued to work for regional unity, citywide outreaches, and unified prayer gatherings. We helped to sponsor The Call, the Justice House of Prayer, the SF House of Prayer, and dozens of other efforts to bring spiritual and practical transformation to our city. We pioneered ministries among unusual groups of people, such as neo-hippies, dance club "ravers," punk rockers, and hip-hoppers. We sent teams to Rainbow Gatherings, Full-moon Festivals, and Burning Man gatherings. In 2007, we gathered hundreds of believers for a major outreach called Summer of Love commemorating the fortieth anniversary of the hippie Summer of Love and the launch of the Jesus People Movement.

There is so much more to say, but I think you get the idea. Destiny often comes in stages, and each stage has its plowing, planting, and harvest seasons.

As I write this, I am almost fifty-five years old, and I am in the midst of a new stage of my destiny fulfillment. Two years ago, in the summer of 2009, my family and I moved to the city of Redding in Northern California to begin a new chapter of our lives. For several years, we had been in fellowship with Bethel Church, which has been a major source of renewal in the Body of Christ for a decade or more. We initially came for a "summer sabbatical" to build deeper relationships with the leaders here, but through God's guidance, we realized that He had another purpose. He wanted us to live here for the foreseeable future and be part of the world-changing ministry that comes out of the Bethel Movement.

Although I remain connected to our church in the city, I am now privileged to serve in two amazing ministries that are right in line with my destiny focus. As I briefly mentioned in an earlier chapter, the first is Jesus Culture, where I serve as the director of development, and the second is Global Legacy, in which I have developed a coaching tool for churches around the world.

My role in Jesus Culture fulfills my calling to touch emerging culture. I am leading a team that is writing training curriculum for youth and college groups, and I am developing a long-term leadership development program called The Culture Project. In my other role, I get to help pastors and churches identify challenges and overcome hindrances to greater increase. In both cases I function as a builder, and in both cases, I get to fulfill my Kingdom passion to prepare God's people for the coming harvest.

In Conclusion

In closing, I urge you to discover who God has made you to be and to remove every obstacle keeping you from that discovery.

I urge you to align yourself with mentors who will call forth the gold within you and help you to bear hundredfold fruit.

I urge you to use the gifts God has given you and to draw friends around you who can help you on your journey. And most of all, I urge you to *enjoy* the journey as you pursue your personal destiny.

DestinyFinder.com

Destiny Finder, the book, is a companion to the DestinyFinder.com website. The site has the Destiny Guide system, which includes three modules with online surveys, templates, access to personal coaching, and much more to help people discover and begin to fulfill their individual destinies.

Go to DestinyFinder.com and get started by taking the Free Trial Destiny Survey to find out your Destiny Orientation. It will give you a glimpse of your primary core trait that shapes your destiny. You can have your friends take the free survey about you as well for added feedback.

DestinyFinder.com... Unlocking your destiny.